A HISTORY OF THE
HOLBECHE
FAMILY
OF WARWICKSHIRE

AND THE

HOLBECH
FAMILY
OF FARNBOROUGH

A HISTORY OF THE
HOLBECHE
FAMILY
OF WARWICKSHIRE

AND THE

HOLBECH
FAMILY
OF FARNBOROUGH

LAURENCE INCE

BREWIN BOOKS

BREWIN BOOKS
56 Alcester Road,
Studley,
Warwickshire,
B80 7LG
www.brewinbooks.com

Published by Brewin Books 2011

A CIP catalogue record for this book is available
from the British Library.

ISBN: 978-1-85858-482-9

Printed by Information Press Limited.

Contents

Holbech.

Holbeech.

Holbech, of Mollington.

Fig 1 The arms of the Holbeche/Holbech family.

Clapham.

Dabridgcourt.

Leigh, of Stoneleigh.

Fig 2a *The arms of some of the families related to the Holbeche family through marriage (Clapham, Dabridgcourt & Leigh).*

Kittermaster.

Cayley, of Coventry.

Parkyns, of Marston Jabbett.

Fig 2b The arms of some of the families related to the Holbeche family through marriage (Kittermaster, Cayley & Parkyns).

Holbeche   Parsons

Fig 3 *Two Holbech coats of arms discovered at Bentley Hall and Widney, Solihull.*

ix

Introduction and Acknowledgements

IT IS with some relief that I compose this, the last section of my work on the Holbeche and Holbech families. In each century from the seventeenth to the twentieth a member of the family has started to research and write a history of the Holbeches. Sadly none of them lived long enough to complete the task. I can only assume that as I married into the family and do not bear the Holbeche name that I have been able to complete the account safely. When I married Janet Holbeche she informed me that she came from an interesting family and asked if I would research and write the history of the family.

As a historian I had many topics that I wanted to explore and was not fully convinced that a family history of the Holbeches would fire me with enthusiasm. However, I could not have been more wrong. Some family matters around six years ago forced me to look at the family's background with a little more diligence. I soon became fascinated with the topic. Some of the personalities detailed in this volume have a national importance that has added interest to what could have been a parochial family history topic. The research into the Holbeche family has meant that I have had to study virtually every major religious topic from the Reformation to the Oxford Movement. It has taken me from the battlefields of the Wars of the Roses in the fifteenth century to the politics of Northern Ireland in the twentieth century. For my journey along this steep learning curve I must thank all the generations of the family.

I should, perhaps, add at this juncture thanks to all the branches of the family including the ones that adopted the spelling of their family name as Holbech. The spelling of the surname has been one of the major stumbling blocks in the writing of this account. In the fifteenth century when the family moved to Warwickshire the spelling of a surname took many forms as heard and written down by clerks.

So members of the family are recorded as Holbeach, Holbech, Holbeche, Holbache, Holbeache and Holbeech. The Holbech family of Stowe Parke in Lincolnshire spelt their name as Holbech on their church monument and pedigree roll but the Heralds on their visitation to Lincolnshire recorded it as Holbeche on their documents. In Fillongley members of the family are recorded as having both Holbech and Holbeche as their surname. Very often a father might use one form while the other form is recorded for his son. Sometimes you can observe no less than three different spellings on various ancient documents for the same person. In this account I have used the name Holbech and Holbeche for the branches of the family. Where a branch of the family has consistently used Holbech then this is the form I have used. This mainly relates to four groups namely, Anthony Holbech and his family in Solihull, the Holbech family of Birchley Hall, the Holbech family of Stowe Park and the Holbech family of Farnborough Hall.

All members of the Holbech and Holbeche family have common ancestors in Fillongley, Warwickshire. In their early history at Fillongley both main surnames are recorded in the family but by the middle of the seventeenth century the accepted form had become Holbeche and for consistency my description of the Fillongley branch will mainly use that form.

This account contains a huge fund of family history. Much of this was gathered by the Rev Gerald Holbeche who completed the Holbeche family tree and had it accepted for the 1952 edition of Burke's Landed Gentry. His researches into the family started in the early 1940s and stretched to the mid 1970s and he was ably helped by Ronald Holbeche of Essex. Additional work on the early history of the family was also completed by Canon Hugh Holbech of Farnborough Hall. I must also thank Geoffrey Holbech, also of Farnborough Hall, for his help, advice and interest in this project. It has been a long held wish by many members of the family that one day an account of this interesting group of Warwickshire people would be published. I have taken up the baton and without their pioneering work I think I would have found the task of writing this family history an impossibility.

I hope they approve of this account and maybe they would be surprised by some of the detail I have managed to unearth regarding the family.

I would not have been able to complete this task without the help of many institutions. I am particularly indebted to the staffs of the Warwickshire County Record Office, the Shakespeare Birthplace Trust Records Office, the Guildhall Library, London and the archives and reference departments of Birmingham Central Library. For permission to use illustrations in this volume I thank the Master and Fellows of Emmanuel College, Cambridge and Stoneleigh Abbey (http://www.stoneleighabbey.org). I am indebted to Peter and Edna Handley of Solihull for advice and their help in providing illustrations for this volume. Various members from different branches of the family have assisted me with this task and I am particularly grateful for information received and help with illustrations from Barnaby and Linda Holbeche and Fay and Charles Butt of Australia.

Chapter One

The Holbeches
of Lincolnshire

THE SECOND half of the fifteenth century was a time of great change for both the country and the Holbeche (Holbech) family. This period was dominated by the Wars of the Roses with its see-saw changes as the Dukes of York and Lancaster alternately gained control of the throne of England. The turbulence of this period left its mark on the family with the death of William Holbeche at the Battle of Towton on Palm Sunday 1461. This battle in Yorkshire has the distinction of being, probably, the largest and bloodiest battle ever fought on English soil. The field was bitterly contested during intense periods of snow and one of the results was a substantial number of casualties. It has been calculated that around 13,000 men died at Towton. Another result of the battle was that with the defeat of the Lancastrians it marked the start of a series of events which led to the coronation of the Yorkist Edward IV as king of England.[i]

Although the Holbeche family had long been settled in Lincolnshire it was Fillongley, in Warwickshire that William Holbeche set out from to travel to the north to take his place at Towton. He went as a retainer of Edward Nevill, Lord Abergavenny. Preserved family pedigrees take the Holbech (Holbeche) family back to 1223 when Oliver of Holbech or de Holbeche lived in Lincolnshire. As the name suggests the family lived and held lands around Holbeach. This was an ancient fenland settlement and the family took its name from where it occupied lands. The name Holbeach comes from the old English words of hol + bece which means hollow stream. The ancient family pedigrees record a series of knights and landowners living in Lincolnshire during medieval times. It is highly likely that a few generations have been missed off this pedigree but with little literacy and no registrations of births and deaths, it is no wonder that these documents are not completely accurate. The pedigrees do record a series of knights called John and Laurence and marriages into the families of other local Lincolnshire gentry. These include the Gedney, Souch, Creasy, Irby (Erby), Branch, Whaplet, Weston, Welby, Moulton (Milton), Pulvertost, Holland and Rochford families. The visitation records for Lincolnshire record Holbeche marriages into these families and records the Holbeche coat of arms as vert, five escallops in saltire argent or more simply as five silver shells on a green background.

There are also records of a monk by the name of Laurence Holbech (Holbeach) who lived at Ramsey Abbey in around 1410. This must be no coincidence as Laurence seems to have been a popular christian name in the family. Laurence Holbech worked on the large number of Hebrew manuscripts at Ramsey and produced the first English – Hebrew dictionary or lexicon and other notable works.

The name de Holbeche occurs as the name of some of the coroners for Lincolnshire. This position needed men to be skilled in law and local government as well as landowners of substance. Not only were they expected to undertake any of the sheriff's duties should the necessity arise but also to perform a number of other tasks. These included the holding of inquests on dead bodies, ensuring the arrest of suspects and the appearance of witnesses in the county court and hearing felon's confessions. In 1300 there were fourteen coroners in Lincolnshire. There seems to have been several branches of the de Holbeches in Lincolnshire. One important member of the family was Sir Laurence de Holbeche who in 1320-21 held manors and lands in Yorkshire and Lincolnshire. His name is recorded with both spellings as de Holbech and de Holbeche. His first wife was Margaret Gumbaud who was the sister of William Gumbaud. Through her de Holbeche held lands in Yorkshire at Thoren Gumbaud, Ottringham and Holm in Holderness. His Lincolnshire estates included land at Trikyngham, Repinghale, Kelingholm, Flete, Kyrkton, Algerkirk and the manor of Holbeach.[ii] The difficult nature of land ownership at Holbeach can be seen in a report that in 1321 one half of the 80 acres of Laurence de Holbeche's land was then under water.[iii] As knights and landowners in Yorkshire and Lincolnshire the Holbeche family must have come under the influence and protection of important members of the northern nobility. In the north and east one of the most important noble families carried the name Nevill and it is to this family that the Holbeches owe their move from Lincolnshire to Warwickshire.

In the reign of King John, Robert Fitzmalden, Lord of Raby and Brancepeth married Isabella de Nevill, the heiress of modest estates in Lincolnshire, Yorkshire and Durham. From then on the Nevill name replaced Fitzmalden. By 1397 Ralph Nevill was so rich and influential that Richard II tried to win his support by granting him the Earldom of Westmorland. Two years later Earl Ralph deserted the king to support his wife's half brother, Henry of Lancaster in his attempt to usurp the throne. Ralph Nevill was richly rewarded for his services at such a critical time.[iv] Ralph Nevill's lands and wealth was increased by his use of wardships and negotiated marriages. Under English law the wardship of any minor who inherited landed property passed automatically to the crown, who normally gave (or sold) it back to the relatives of the child or some other favoured applicant. The guardian was then free to enjoy the income from the property until the minor came of age, by which time he would have either sold his ward's marriage to the highest bidder or have arranged a marriage within his own family circle. In about 1400-1401, Ralph, Lord Nevill and Earl of Westmorland granted Ralph de Rochford the wardship of John de Holbeche and his lands in Lincolnshire. So here we see the intimate connection between the Holbeches and the Nevill family. The Holbeche family pedigrees also record other familiar links with the Rochford family whose members often occupied the position of Sheriff of Lincoln.

Nevill land ownership was increased when Edward Nevill became Lord Abergavenny. The Nevills had inherited the Lordship of Abergavenny from the Beauchamps. Richard Beauchamp had died in 1417 and left an only child, Elizabeth who married Sir Edward Nevill. For some time Sir Edward and his wife were kept out of the lordship by Richard Beauchamp, Earl of Warwick and his son, Henry, Duke of Warwick. However, Sir Edward Nevill gained the confidence of King Edward IV and became possessed of the manor and was summoned to Parliament in 1450 as Baron de Bergavenny.

The lordship of Abergavenny had at one time been held by the Hastings family and included other properties dotted around England.[v] One of these was the manor of Fillongley in Warwickshire. It would have been important that the Nevills had their own men in place to oversee their new manors. At Fillongley it was to the Holbeche (Holbech) family that Nevill turned to for help. Perhaps it was with an exchange or grant of land that encouraged the move to Warwickshire. As well as land the family received important positions such as reeve and bailiff of the Abergavenny estate. The Holbeche family were soon interacting with the other important families in the Fillongley area such as the Sadlers and Brearleys. The first documentary evidence of the Holbeche family residing in Warwickshire is the Register of the Guild of Knowle, when John Holbeche and his wife, Alice are listed as members in 1460.[vi] In 1483 his nephew, Thomas Holbeche and his wife Alice were recorded as members. At this time Richard Brearley was Master of the Guild and a member of the Holbeche family was married to a Brearley. Several representatives of other important Fillongley families were also members of the Guild of Knowle.

Edward Nevill, Lord Abergavenny played an important role in government during the Wars of the Roses. He was the fifth and youngest son of Ralph, Earl of Westmorland and Joan Beaufort. Edward was, like his elder brothers, a supporter of his brother-in-law Richard of York. Edward's first documented appearance in the Wars of the Roses was in 1460 when he joined his brothers, Salisbury and Fauconberg, and his nephews, Edward of March and Richard of Warwick on their return from exile. Edward was present at the Battle of Northampton and in 1461 he was again present with his nephew Edward of March at the Battle of Mortimer's Cross. After Edward of March was proclaimed king Abergavenny supported him at the bloody Battle of Towton. The Battles of Barnet and Tewkesbury once again saw Abergavenny at the king's side, even though at Barnet it meant that he took sides against his other nephews, Warwick and Montagu.

During his lifetime Abergavenny held offices both under the houses of Lancaster and York. He was several times appointed commissioner of array for

Kent, being chief commissioner in 1471. He was also a privy councillor in York's protectorate in 1454. He died in 1476. It was Edward Nevill's role and inheritance that saw William Holbeche present on the Towton battlefield in 1461 and it also explains the presence of the Holbeche family in Fillongley during the second half of the fifteenth century.

---

[i]   Christopher Gravett, *Towton 1461, England's Bloodiest Battle* (Botley, 2003).

[ii] *Calendar Of Inquisitions*, Edward II, Writ 21 April, 14 Edward II for Laurence de Holbech, pp. 164-165.

[iii] Graham Platts, *History of Lincolnshire, Vol. IV, Land and People in Medieval Lincolnshire* (Lincoln, 1985), p. 118.

[iv] J.R. Lander, *Crown and Nobility 1450 – 1509*, (1976), p. 95.

[v]   Sir Joseph Bradney, *A History of Monmouthshire, Volume 1, The Hundred of Abergavenny* (1906), pp. 146 – 152.

[vi] W.B. Bickley (Editor), *The Register of the Guild of Knowle* (Walsall, 1894), p. 33.

Plate 1 All Saints Church, Holbeach, Lincolnshire. This church was built in the fourteenth century. Before this rebuilding the Holbeche family owned the advowson for the parish for a brief period.

Plate 2 This entrance porch for All Saints Church, Holbeach is said to be a re-use of the entrance gate for the manor house of the Moulton family. The daughter of Sir Thomas Moulton married Sir Laurence Holbeche (born c.1355).

Plate 3 St Mary's Church, Whaplode. This important medieval church near Holbeach holds an important Irby (Erby) family tomb.

Plate 4 The Irby tomb in St Mary's Church, Whaplode. This seventeenth century tomb contains the
remains of Sir Anthony (1576-1610) and Lady Elizabeth Irby. The Irby family are typical of the
Lincolnshire landed gentry that the Holbeche family associated with before their move to Warwickshire.
In the fifteenth century Richard Holbeche (b. c1416) married Cassandra Irby.

Chapter Two

Fillongley and the Holbeche Family

SOON THE Holbeche family were settled into their new Warwickshire surroundings. As important estate officers for Lord Abergavenny they held a prominent position in Fillongley society. It was not long before they were marrying into other important gentry families in the area such as with the Sadler and Brearley families. The Holbeche family became prominent landowners in the area and occupied many of the important houses to be found around Fillongley. Members of the Holbeche family in the sixteenth and seventeenth centuries were to be found occupying the White House, Fillongley Hall, Birchley Hall and the Manor House in Fillongley. At this time members of the family living close to Fillongley had their names recorded in various ways including Holbach, Holbeche and Holbech. By the middle of the seventeenth century most members of the family around Fillongley were consistently using Holbeche as their surname.

One important branch of the Holbeche family lived in the White House. This house was in the possession of William Holbeche who died in 1558. The Holbeche family had arrived in Warwickshire with a coat of arms, namely five silver shells or escallops on a green background. The shells could indicate pilgrimage or being present on a crusade. William Holbeche was allowed to change the family's coat of arms for his own use and for his descendants. He changed the number of shells from five to six and it is tradition in the family that he was allowed to do this due to his prowess in war. Certainly in his will he bequeathed to his six sons all the 'Harnesse and weapons he had belonging to the king's wars' but his cross-bow with the rack went to his son Martin.[i] Although several of his descendants adopted the six shells coat of arms other groups continued to use the five shells. William Holbeche held a considerable amount of land around Fillongley including copyhold tenements in the manor which had previously been in the possession of his brother. After William's death they were held by his son Martin. William Holbeche had married Elizabeth Petye of Tetsworth and Henley, Oxfordshire. He was buried at Fillongley on 26 August 1558. He is described in his will as of, 'Yonge Fillongley' and asked to be buried, 'in the new aisle at the door coming into the said aisle from the body of the church as may be convenient'. His will was dated 1557.

The Holbeches in the sixteenth century were landowners and farmers. In their wills they are often described as yeomen. William Holbeche's brother, Leonard died in 1546 with his will proved 30th April 1547. He is described as dying at the time of plague. The influence of farming and duty to the church is easily discerned in the following extract from his will. Leonard Holbeche asked, 'To be buried in the church of Fyllongley. To the high altar 8d. To the reparation and maintenance of the church goods a tablecloth of flax. I give 5s to be spent on wax at my burial. I give 40s to be spent on meat and drink upon my neighbours and poor people on the day of my burial. To the poor people of Arley, Astley and Corley, 5s. To Elizabeth Wood, William Holbeche, son of Barnaby, John Brearley, son of Elizabeth Brearley and to Leonard Osmond, son of Richmond Osmond and to William Holbeche son of John Holbeche Junior, to every of them a lamb of this year and to all other godchildren 4d a piece. To the reparation of the highway, there is most need, 6s 8d. To Thomas Eddes, a jacket. I will that Agnes, my wife, shall have 8 kine, a bull and a mare. I will that Margaret Perkyns be paid her part of her legacy of her father's gift out of my whole goods. Residue to Agnes my wife and to John Holbeche my son exactly between them whom I make them my executors'.[ii]

Sheep farming certainly played an important part in the local agricultural economy. The will of John Holbeche of 26 July 1561 stated that, 'Every one of my servants should receive a sheep and to Thomas Holbeche my brother Thomas' son ten sheep'. In fact a Thomas Holbeche is named as a sheep breeder on his marriage to Elizabeth Matthew of Mercotte Hall, Berkswell. The wool industry was an important generator of revenue for the whole of the country. During downturns in the industry, the government realising the importance of the trade, often intervened. In the late seventeenth century in an effort to boost wool production the government insisted that people should be buried in woollen not linen shrouds. In April 1690 it was recorded that Dame Ester Caley, a relative of the Holbeches was buried with a woollen shroud.

As the Holbeche family grew and took over more land in the Fillongley area so opportunities for some members of the family became limited. One member of the family that moved from Fillongley at an early juncture was Thomas Holbech. He returned to Lincolnshire to live at Stowe Park. Thomas Holbech was another member of the family that had acquitted himself well in the service of the king. It is recorded that, 'At the siege of the French cities of Montreuil and Boulogne in 1544, Thomas Holbech, a very brave man, carried off the prize from his comrades, for Henry VIII added to his family arms, which consisted of five shells, three golden lions' heads to be borne on an azure ground, as a special reward for the valour which he displayed'. In fact it was this member of the family that asked the Heralds to look into his Lincolnshire roots and to draw up a pedigree. He married Anne Yaxley of Yaxley Mellis, Suffolk and died 15 April 1591. A stone tablet in St Mary's Church, Stow commemorates his and his wife's lives. The shield that is present on this memorial proudly bears the five shells and the three lions granted by the king for valour. Unfortunately this branch of the family became extinct after two further generations. However, Thomas Holbech of Stow must be praised as being the first member of the family to try and record the family history.

While Thomas was spending time investigating his Lincolnshire background, members of the family continued as bailiffs and stewards to the manor of Fillongley. As late as the 1690s Thomas Holbeche was named as steward and bailiff to the lord of the manor of Fillongley. He also acted as the Coroner for the area.[iii]

The middle of the sixteenth century saw great changes in religion and land ownership when Henry VIII transformed the country from a Catholic one into a

Protestant one. He founded the Church of England and also dissolved the monasteries. From the preserved records members of the Holbeche family appear to have accepted the changes and embraced the new religion with family members still holding local offices such as the position of churchwarden. Although most members of the family served the community well there are some incidents of Holbeches over stepping the mark. In Easter 1649 Amilion Holbeche had to present himself at the Quarter Sessions. He was charged that he had pretended to be the bailiff of the manor of Fillongley under Lord Abergavenny. Acting in this way he had seized and taken away all the goods and cattle of Morris Halfield and Thomas Archer to the value of about thirty pounds upon the pretence that they had committed felonies. He had also under false pretences taken from widow Walker a cow and divers goods from Elizabeth Belcher and George Dunton. Amilion Holbeche was bound over to keep the peace and pay Archer 18d a week.[iv] In 1650 he was not paying this sum and was warned by the court.[v] What his relatives Edward and Thomas Holbeche, who had recently been elected as churchwardens, thought of Amilion's actions can only be imagined.

These were turbulent times with the political arguments of the 1630s and early 1640s developing into the English Civil War of 1642-1649. Laud, Archbishop of Canterbury was pushing through many changes in the Church of England making it more like the Catholic church. Perhaps this is why Thomas Holbeche was presented at the Easter Quarter Sessions at Warwick in 1635 for being absent from church for three months.[vi] Generally the Holbeche family appear to have been more sympathetic to the Parliamentarian rather than the Royalist cause. Certainly the family had strong links with the Parliamentary cause. Edward Holbeche (d. 1670) had married Frances Hesilrige. She was the sister of Sir Arthur Hesilrige of Alderton, Northamptonshire.[vii] Arthur Hesilrige was a great Parliamentary leader and one of the five 'birds' that had to flee Parliament from the wrath of Charles I. This was one of the defining moments of the last Parliament before the Civil War broke out.[viii]

Another important parliamentary sympathiser in the family was Martin Holbeche (1597-1670). He was the second of three sons of George Holbeche and Millicent, daughter of John Poultney of Exhall near Coventry. Martin was admitted a pensioner at Queen's College, Cambridge on 24 September 1617 to be later joined by his brother, Gabriel. He matriculated in 1621 and graduated BA in 1622. Martin Holbeche was ordained as a deacon in London during 1624 and proceeded to an MA in 1625. He later taught at Braintree and Halstead. In 1627 he was appointed master of Felsted School by Robert Rich, second Earl of Warwick. While at university Holbeche met Thomas Hooker and had become a member of Hooker's local fraternity of godly ministers, many of whom were at odds with the direction being taken by the Church of England under Laud. Martin Holbeche had a distinguished teaching career and Felsted School grew apace. Pupil numbers rose from 100 to 120 and the school attracted notable patrons. Pupils included the four sons of Oliver Cromwell and Henry Mildmay (1619-1692), later MP for Essex. Holbeche prospered at Felsted and he bought Lawsells, the largest house in Felsted. In 1638 the Earl of Essex raised his salary to £50 a year. After the Restoration John Bramston claimed that Holbeche 'scarce bred any man that was loyal to his prince'. Holbeche had a reputation in godly quarters such that on 17 June 1643 the House of Commons resolved to place in his charge the two sons of the third Lord Arundell of Wardour who were parliament's prisoners. In May 1644 the boys were exchanged for the grandsons of the Earl of Warwick who had been captured by the king's forces.

In the late 1640s Martin Holbeche's developing Independent convictions led to a rift with his, then, patron the Earl of Essex. He left Felsted School at Christmas 1649. In 1654 Holbeche was appointed an assistant to the county commission of triers and ejectors. In 1661 Martin Holbeche was again at odds with the newly restored Church of England. He was ejected from his living and he moved back to Felsted. He died at Dunmow on 30 September 1670.[ix]

Although other members of the family had some royalist leanings it seems that few if any of the family took part in any actual fighting. During the seventeenth century the Holbeche family managed to extend their land holdings around Fillongley through marriages and prudent purchases. One important marriage was that of Thomas Holbeche to Elizabeth Matthew of Mercotte Hall, Meriden. There had been a long association with the family and this area for in the reign of Mary, John Holbech was holding land at Meriden.[x] Thomas Holbeche was described as a sheep breeder from Fillongley. After his marriage to Elizabeth Matthew he bought Meriden Hall and the surrounding fields in 1614. Thomas

Holbeche left Meriden Manor to his younger sons Matthew (1606-1663) and Martin (1615-1688). Both were trained as lawyers. Matthew became Recorder at Warwick and did not live at the hall after his marriage to Ann Hales. Martin, a bachelor did, acting as agent for his brother. He was also consulted by residents who were drawing up legal contracts. Martin was also interested in local history and became a close friend to William Dugdale, the great Warwickshire antiquary. He was also a successful sheep and cattle breeder. The last male member of this branch of the family died in 1713.[xi]

Another important marriage was to catapult the Holbeche family into the forefront of Warwickshire society. This was the marriage in the mid seventeenth century of Thomas Holbeche to Elizabeth Daniels. He was a member of the Fillongley Hall Holbeches and she was the only surviving granddaughter and co-heiress of Bernard Paulet, the great grandson of Giles Paulet of Cokels, Wiltshire, the fourth son of the first Marquis of Winchester. The Paulet family held much land in Warwickshire including the manor of Maxstoke. In 1331 William de Clinton, Earl of Huntingdon established a chantry at Maxstoke, subsequently transferring the endowment to found a house of Augustinian canons. The priory lordship was granted in 1538 to Charles, Duke of Suffolk who in 1540 sold it to Robert Trapps of London. The manor passed to Nicholas Trapps who died in 1544 leaving two daughters. One of these married Giles Paulet, the son of the Marquess of Winchester. The Paulets continued to hold Maxstoke until 1706. This estate would have been inherited by Elizabeth Daniels but it was used as the marriage settlement for her daughter Mary Holbeche. She married on 11 September 1705, Edward 3rd Baron Leigh of Stoneleigh and brought with her a considerable dowry. The estates consisted of Maxstoke Priory, rectories at Shustoke, Bentley, Fillongley all in Warwickshire and an estate at Nosterfield Priors in Cambridgeshire. This large dowry allowed the Leigh family to build a towering baroque house in front of the earlier Elizabethan house which in 1626 already was the largest house in Warwickshire. Mary Holbeche's father and other relatives were allowed to occupy Maxstoke Priory which became the family home. When Thomas Holbeche occupied Maxstoke Priory he had to spend much money in restoring the building which appears not to have been lived in for a considerable amount of time. The repairs came to a total of £68 12s 2d and included the costs for spars, boards for the Great Gates, planks and nails. Seven men worked at the Priory at between 8d to 14d a day.[xii] When Thomas Holbeche died in 1705 Maxstoke Priory consisted of a study, chamber, a chamber over the pantry, the little chamber, the chamber over the hall, the chamber over the Great Parlour, men's chamber, chamber over the servants' hall, closet in the kitchen chamber, garret over the great parlour, chamber over the little parlour, garret over the little parlour, hall chamber, kitchen, hall, pantry, Great Parlour, Little Parlour, Servants' Hall, Brewhouse, dairy, cellar, Little Cockloft, Great Cockloft and a maids' chamber.[xiii]

During the seventeenth century pressure on Holbeche land saw several groups from the family leave the Fillongley area to seek their fortune in other areas of Warwickshire. Holbeches were soon to be found at Mollington on the Oxfordshire/Warwickshire borders, at Birchley Hall, Corley and Stoneleigh and in the area around Solihull and Knowle. This had an adverse effect for in the middle of the eighteenth century the Holbeche presence in the Fillongley area was beginning to look decidedly thin. The last member of the Holbeche family of the White House died in 1745. This was Edward Holbeche who was unmarried and left the majority of his estate including the White House to his friend William Dilke of Maxstoke Castle.[xiv]

The last branch of the family in the Fillongley area was the Holbeche family of Fillongley Hall. Thomas Holbeche had leased out Fillongley Hall and occupied Maxstoke Priory. As we have seen Thomas Holbeche expended a large sum in restoring Maxstoke Priory and his son, Aemillian is later described as being of Maxstoke Priory. During the occupation of Maxstoke Priory Aemillian Holbeche experienced a breakdown in his marriage. He was married to Mary Vincent. In legal papers Aemillian was described as a goldsmith of the City of London. It was quite common for members of the family to look forward to inheriting property but they were also put out to learn a trade. An agreement concerning a separation and the division of the estate of Aemillian Holbeche was reached in 10th June 1758.[xv] This was brokered by a member of the Holbech family of Farnborough Hall and Aemillian's nephew Thomas Holbeche of Hill Court, Dodderhill, Worcestershire. The family network continued to work even though they were now dotted around the county. For some time Thomas Holbeche was considered to be head of the family. He was a lawyer and had married Dorothy Penrice the daughter of the vicar of Dodderhill. It was this marriage that brought Thomas Holbeche to the Droitwich area. He was a well known lawyer and magistrate in Droitwich and was also solicitor to the Droitwich Canal. Marriage into the Penrice family brought him the advowson of St. Augustine's Church at Dodderhill. All his children by Dorothy died at a young age and their lives are commemorated in a stone tablet in St Augustine's Church, Dodderhill. Dorothy Holbeche died in 1771 and Thomas Holbeche married again. His second wife was Christian Amphlett the widow of William Amphlett of Hadzor who was High Sheriff of Worcester. She died in 1807 and was buried at Hadzor. Thomas Holbeche was also buried at Hadzor.

Two more generations continued to live in the Fillongley area. The last Holbeche at Fillongley was Aemillian of Slowley Hill. Perhaps this member of the family was not the most trustworthy of the clan. He married Catherine Smith of Berkeswell in 1817 and the marriage settlement really made sure that he would not have access to her fortune. He was to have the interest during his life but on his death the dowry would revert to his wife and on his death she received all his chattels and goods.[xvi] Aemillian died in 1833 leaving some problems behind him. This revolved around the management of William Avery's Charity at Fillongley. Avery had left land and money for the education of boys and their later apprenticeship in the world of work. However, a descendent of Avery went to litigation in an attempt to regain some of this property. The Holbeche family had been involved in the charity for many years and it was left to Aemillian Holbeche to fight a protracted court case which he won. As he had expended money on litigation the trustees allowed him to occupy lands owned by the charity and to receive rents till he was reimbursed. However, it was twenty years before any more income became available for the charity. Account books were only kept from 1810 onwards and Aemillian Holbeche as bailiff occupied Slowley Hill Farm one of the charity's major possessions. Also from the year 1815 very large balances, sometimes approaching £350 remained in the bailiff's hand without earning interest. Because of the increase of income Aemillian Holbeche had doubled his own salary. This all became apparent on the death of Aemillian in 1833.[xvii] Perhaps Aemillian's high handed ways prompted Thomas, his brother, to move his family away in the late eighteenth century to Sutton Coldfield to start a new chapter in the life of the Holbeche family. When Aemillian's widow Catherine died in 1847 she left little to the Holbeche side of her family.[xviii]

Although no Holbeche family members now live in Fillongley there are many reminders of the name in the district. Holbeche Crescent skirts around the side of the churchyard and the church contains many reminders of the family's service to the parish. There is a large board in the church which records all the donations made to local charities and the Holbeche name figures on it several times. Francis Holbeche of Fillongley and Thomas Holbeche of Meriden were early benefactors to the parish. In 1748 the Butt Fields' Charity was set up. Money was donated to purchase Butt Fields which consisted of 15 acres and cost £170. The list of donors included six Holbeche family members.[xix] Some earlier donations were consolidated around this charity including the gift from Widow Holbeche of £10. The interest from this sum was to be given in bread on the 30th June, 'to such of the poor who came oftenest to church and behaved themselves best'. There are also in the church two large monuments to the family. One is a late eighteenth century monument recording the lives and deaths of Mary and Aemillian Holbeche and their family. The second monument is dated 1725 and records the death of Anne Daniels and her daughter Elizabeth who was married to Thomas Holbeche. It was their daughter, Mary who married Lord Leigh, Baron of Stoneleigh. It was Lord Leigh who caused the monument to be erected. In the chancel of the church were flat stones that commemorated at least seven members of the Holbeche family.[xx] There are also fragments of a Holbeche window. This is in the north window of the Lady Chapel. The fragments are of Dutch origin and were rescued from a window in the old Manor House when it was destroyed by fire in 1929. These fragments came from a Holbeche family window and mentions Willem, Elizabeth Averay his wife, Aemilion Holbeache and Thomas Holbeache. Also present in the fragments is the representation of a horned ram and at the head of the window is a picture of a father leading his family in prayer. The names recorded on the glass would indicate a mid-seventeenth century date for the window. The tower of the church at Fillongley contains eight bells and one has a Holbeche inscription. It is inscribed 'Soli Deo Gloria In Pax Hominibus. Edward Holbach, Thomas Brealie. 1654'. Many of the churchwardens at Fillongley were members of the Holbeche family and their generosity and piety is recorded in the church by their gifts to local charities and the part purchase of a bell. Some of these gifts became a Holbeche Charity which has now united with all the other Fillongley charities. This continues the family tradition of piety and charitable work into the twenty first century.

---

[i] *Burke's Landed Gentry*, (1952), Holbeche of Hillybroom, p. 1255.

[ii] Warwickshire Record Office, Holbeche Family Papers, CR/1680/632, 3, Abstract of Will of Leonard Holbache of Fillongley, dated 13th August 1546.

[iii] H.C. Johnson & N.J. Williams (Eds.), *Warwick County Records, Volume IX, Quarter Session Records, Easter 1690 to Michaelmas 1696* (Warwick, 1964), p. 5 & p. 131.

[iv] S.C. Ratcliffe & H.C. Johnson, *Warwick County Records, Volume II, Quarter Sessions Order Book, Michaelmas 1637 to Epiphany 1650*, (Warwick, 1936), p. 233.

[v] S.C. Ratcliffe & H.C. Johnson, *Warwick County Records, Volume III, Quarter Sessions Order Book, Easter 1650 to Epiphany 1657*, (Warwick, 1960), p. 7 & p. 24.

[vi] S.C. Ratcliffe & H.C. Johnson, *Warwick County Records, Volume VI, Quarter Sessions, Indictment Book, Easter 1631 to Epiphany 1674*, (Warwick, 1941), p. 34.

[vii] Warwickshire Record Office, Fetherston-Dilke of Maxstoke Collection, Miscellaneous Deeds and Papers, CR 2981/Dining Room/Wooden Chest/Box 22/11, late 17th century.

[viii] Barry Denton, *Only in Heaven, The Life and Campaigns of Sir Arthur Hesilrige, 1601-1661* (Sheffield, 1997).

[ix] *NDNB*, Vivienne Larminie, Martin Holbeach (Holbech), schoolmaster and ejected minister, (Oxford, 2004-5). Michael Craze, *A History of Felsted School 1564 – 1947*, (Ipswich, 1955), pp. 50-64.

[x] William Dugdale, *The Antiquities of Warwickshire* (1656), p. 721.

[xi] Doreen M.K. Agutter, *Meriden: Its People and Houses* (ND), p. 49.

[xii] Shakespeare Birthplace Trust Records Office, Leigh of Stoneleigh, DR 18/3/35/8a, Account of Expenses in Repairs of the Priory and Buildings.

[xiii] Shakespeare Birthplace Trust Records Office, Leigh of Stoneleigh, DR 18/4/8, Inventory of Goods and Chattels and Credits of Thomas Holbeche, Fifth Year of the Reign of Queen Anne.

[xiv] Warwickshire Record Office, Holbeche Family Papers, CR 1680/632, 24, Will of Edward Holbech of Fillongley, Gentleman, dated 10 July, 1745.

[xv] Warwickshire Record Office, LI/171, Articles of Agreement dividing of sole and personal estate between Aemillian Holbeche, Thomas Holbeche, Elizabeth Holbeche, children of Aemillian and Mary, 10 June 1758.

[xvi] Warwickshire Record Office, Bree of Allesley and Beausale Estate Paper, Holbeche of Arley, CR 1709/249/1, Marriage Settlement of Catherine Smith and Amilian Holbeche, 6 January 1817.

[xvii] *Parliamentary Papers, An Act for appointing Commissioners to continue the Inquiries concerning Charities in England and Wales for Two Years and from thence to the End of the next Session of Parliament* (1835), pp. 942-945.

[xviii] Warwickshire Record Office, Bree of Allesley and Beausale Estate Papers, Holbeche of Arley, CR 1709/249/5-25, Probate of the Will of Catherine Holbeche of Berkswell, widow, 1847.

[xix] Parliamentary Papers (1835), pp. 946-951.

[xx] William Dugdale, *The Antiquities of Warwickshire* (2nd Edition, 1730), Vol II, p. 1036.

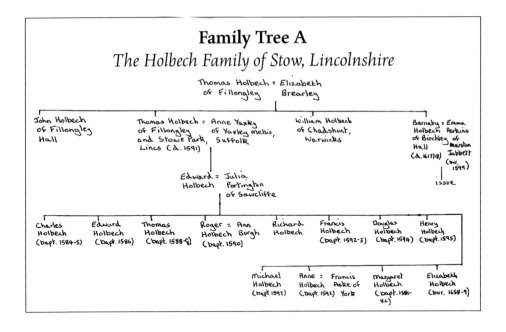

Family Tree A
The Holbech Family of Stow, Lincolnshire

Thomas Holbech = Elizabeth
of Fillongley   Brearley

John Holbech of Fillongley Hall

Thomas Holbech of Fillongley and Stowe Park, Lincs (d. 1591) = Anne Yaxley of Yaxley mellis, Suffolk

William Holbech of Chadshunt, Warwicks

Barnaby Holbech of Birchley Hall (d. 1617/18) = Emma Perkins of Marston Jabbett (bur. 1599)

issue

Edward Holbech = Julia Portington of Sawcliffe

Charles Holbech (bapt. 1584-5)

Edward Holbech (bapt. 1586)

Thomas Holbech (bapt. 1588-9)

Roger Holbech (bapt. 1590) = Ann Burgh

Richard Holbech

Francis Holbech (bapt. 1592-3)

Douglas Holbech (bapt. 1594)

Henry Holbech (bapt. 1595)

Michael Holbech (bapt. 1591)

Anne Holbech (bapt. 1592) = Francis Aske of York

Margaret Holbech (bapt. 1581-82)

Elizabeth Holbech (bur. 1658-9)

Family Tree B
The Holbeches of the White House, Fillongley

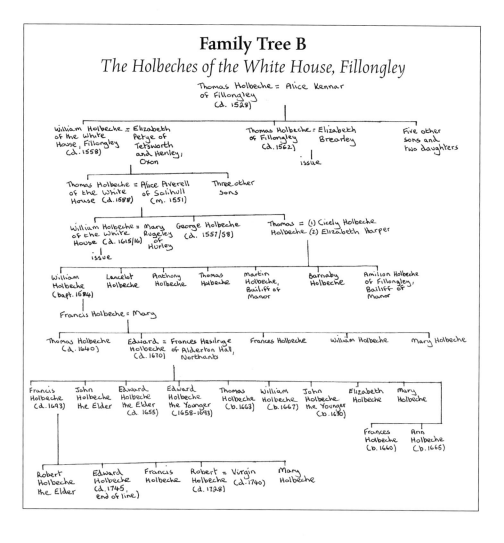

Thomas Holbeche = Alice Kennar
of Fillongley
(d. 1528)

William Holbeche = Elizabeth
of the White   Petye of
House, Fillongley   Tetsworth
(d. 1558)   and Henley,
                     Oxon

Thomas Holbeche = Elizabeth
of Fillongley   Brearley
(d. 1562)
                     issue

Five other
sons and
two daughters

Thomas Holbeche = Alice Averell
of the White   of Solihull
House (d. 1588)   (m. 1551)

Three other
sons

William Holbeche = Mary   George Holbeche   Thomas = (1) Cicely Holbeche
of the White   Rugeley   (d. 1557/58)   Holbeche (2) Elizabeth Harper
House (d. 1615/16) of
                  Hurley
issue

William   Lancelot   Anthony   Thomas   Martin   Barnaby   Amilion Holbeche
Holbeche   Holbeche   Holbeche   Holbeche   Holbeche,   Holbeche   of Fillongley,
(bapt. 1584)   Bailiff of   Bailiff of
                                                   Manor   Manor

Francis Holbeche = Mary

Thomas Holbeche   Edward = Frances Hesilrige   Frances Holbeche   William Holbeche   Mary Holbeche
(d. 1640)   Holbeche of Alderton Hall,
                     (d. 1670) Northants

Francis   John   Edward   Edward   Thomas   William   John   Elizabeth   Mary
Holbeche   Holbeche   Holbeche   Holbeche   Holbeche   Holbeche   Holbeche   Holbeche   Holbeche
(d. 1693)   the Elder   the Elder   the Younger (b. 1663) (b. 1667) the Younger
                          (d. 1655)   (1658-1693)   (b. 1670)

                                                                                       Frances   Ann
                                                                                       Holbeche   Holbeche
                                                                                       (b. 1660)   (b. 1665)

Robert   Edward   Francis   Robert = Virgin   Mary
Holbeche   Holbeche   Holbeche   Holbeche (d. 1740)   Holbeche
the Elder   (d. 1745,   (d. 1728)
               end of line)

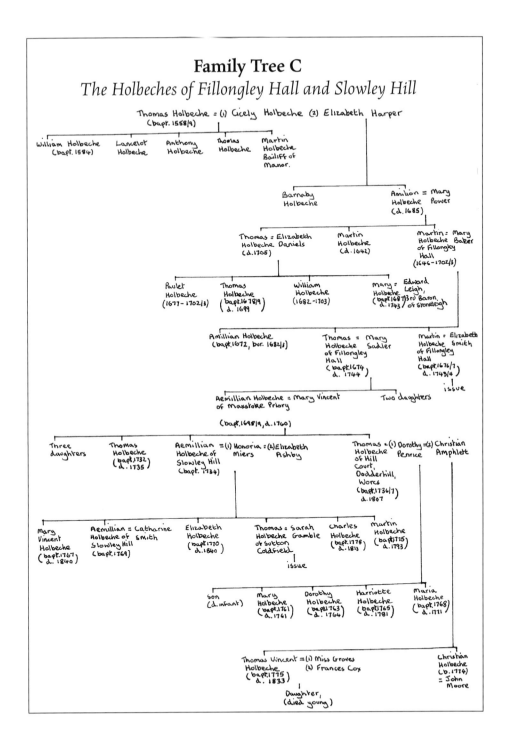

Family Tree C
The Holbeches of Fillongley Hall and Slowley Hill

Thomas Holbeche = (1) Cicely Holbeche (2) Elizabeth Harper
(bapt. 1558/9)

William Holbeche (bapt. 1584) — Lancelot Holbeche — Anthony Holbeche — Thomas Holbeche — Martin Holbeche Bailiff of Manor.

Barnaby Holbeche

Amilion = Mary Holbeche Power (d. 1685)

Thomas = Elizabeth Holbeche Daniels (d. 1705) — Martin Holbeche (d. 1642) — Martin = Mary Holbeche Baker of Fillongley Hall (1646-1702/3)

Paulet Holbeche (1677-1702/3) — Thomas Holbeche (bapt. 1678/9 d. 1699) — William Holbeche (1682-1703) — Mary = Edward Holbeche Leigh, (bapt. 1673 d. 1743) 3rd Baron of Stoneleigh

Amillian Holbeche (bapt. 1672, bur. 1682/3) — Thomas = Mary Holbeche Sadler of Fillongley Hall (bapt. 1674 d. 1744) — Martin = Elizabeth Holbeche Smith of Fillongley Hall (bapt. 1676/7 d. 1743/4) issue

Aemillian Holbeche = Mary Vincent of Maxstoke Priory (bapt. 1698/9, d. 1760) — Two daughters

Three daughters — Thomas Holbeche (bapt. 1732 d. 1735) — Aemillian = (1) Honoria = (2) Elizabeth Holbeche of Miers Ashby Slowley Hill (bapt. 1734) — Thomas = (1) Dorothy = (2) Christian Holbeche Penrice Amphlett of Hill Court, Dodderhill, Worcs (bapt. 1736/7) d. 1807

Mary Vincent Holbeche (bapt. 1767 d. 1840) — Aemillian = Catharine Holbeche of Smith Slowley Hill (bapt. 1769) — Elizabeth Holbeche (bapt. 1770 d. 1840) — Thomas = Sarah Holbeche Gamble of Sutton Coldfield issue — Charles Holbeche (bapt. 1778 d. 1813) — Martin Holbeche (bapt. 1775 d. 1793)

son (d. infant) — Mary Holbeche (bapt. 1761 d. 1761) — Dorothy Holbeche (bapt. 1763 d. 1764) — Harriotte Holbeche (bapt. 1765 d. 1781) — Maria Holbeche (bapt. 1768 d. 1771)

Thomas Vincent = (1) Miss Groves Holbeche (2) Frances Cox (bapt. 1775 d. 1833) — Daughter, (died young) — Christian Holbeche (b. 1774) = John Moore

Family Tree D
The Holbeches of Fillongley

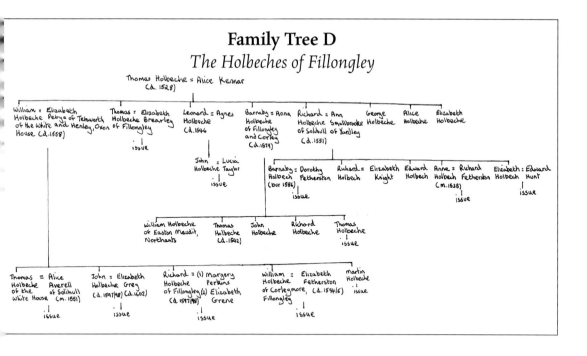

Plate 5 Saint Mary and All Saints Church, Fillongley. This important medieval church in Warwickshire contains many Holbeche monuments.

Plate 6 Mid-seventeenth century glass re-used in Fillongley Church. These fragments were rescued from a window in the old Manor House when it was destroyed by fire in 1929. The window recorded members of the Holbeche family living in Fillongley.

Plate 7 Another glass panel saved from the old Manor House in Fillongley. This shows, possibly, a father and his children in prayer.

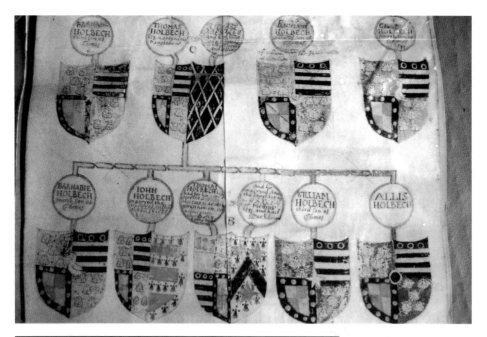

Plate 8 Part of a
seventeenth century
pedigree roll which shows
the descent of the
Holbeche family.

Plate 9 One of the
Holbeche monuments in
St Mary and All Saints
Church, Fillongley.

Plate 10 Maxstoke Priory, home for one branch of the Holbeche family in the early eighteenth century.

Plate 11 Mary Holbeche (1687-1743). Her marriage to Edward Leigh, third Baron of Stoneleigh took the Maxstoke Priory estate to the Leigh family. (By permission of Stoneleigh Abbey)

Plate 12 *The older part of Stoneleigh Abbey, this was a conversion
from the original monastic buildings.*

Plate 13 *The new Stoneleigh Abbey built in the early eighteenth century
from the money that came from the Holbeche marriage.*

Plate 14 *Stained glass in Stoneleigh Abbey commemorating the marriage between the Leigh and Holbeche families.*

Plate 15 *Saint Mary's Church, Stow-in-Lindsey.*

Plate 16 Part of the stone tablet commemorating the Holbech family in Stow church. The five shells can be plainly seen as can the three lions granted for valour.

Plate 17 Saint Augustine's Church, Dodderhill, Droitwich.

Plate 18 A memorial tablet to the first wife and children of Thomas Holbeche, St Augustine's, Dodderhill.

Plate 19 A charity board at St Augustine's Church, Dodderhill. The board shows a bequest settled on the church through Thomas Holbeche's estate.

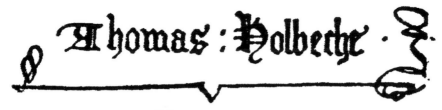

Thomas Holbeche.

Fig 4 The signature of Thomas Holbeche of Fillongley. This has been taken from a deed of entail made 14 December, 1612 by Sir Thomas Dilke, Kt, upon the first marriage of his son with the daughter of Sir Edward Devereux, Kt of Castle Bromwich.

Chapter Three

The Holbech Family
of Birchley Hall

ONE IMPORTANT branch of the Holbech family became established at Birchley Hall near Corley in Warwickshire. The first member of the family to live there was Barnaby Holbech (d. 1617/18). He married Emma Perkins of Marston Jabbett. It was probably this marriage that prompted the move and perhaps supplied the money for the relocation. The Perkins family were considerable landowners at Marston Jabbett until 1696 when Sir William Perkins was executed for high treason and his lands confiscated. However, these lands were later restored to his widow by the king[i].

The second Holbech at Birchley Hall was William who died in 1632. He married three times, the first wife was Francisca Tonge of Ashley, Warwickshire and secondly he married Maria Coloverwell of Cherie Burton, Yorkshire. This second wife was the start of a close association of this family with Yorkshire. His third wife was named Ester. He had seven children. Two of the boys were able to proceed to university at Cambridge. Barnaby (b. 1602) was admitted to Emmanuel College in 1618 and later trained to be a lawyer at Gray's Inn. His brother, Thomas Holbech arrived at Emmanuel in 1622. He matriculated in 1622 obtaining a BA in 1625-26 and an MA in 1629. He became a Bachelor of Divinity in 1636 having been a Fellow of Emmanuel since 1629[ii]. He was known at Cambridge as a man of means. The colleges at Cambridge had Puritan leanings and this was at odds with the ideas of Thomas Holbech. He was one of two fellows of the college identified to the Long Parliament as personae non gratae because they set a dangerous example through bowing at ingress and egress out of the chapel and at the mention of the name of Jesus. His views led him to be forced out of Emmanuel and he took up the position as Vicar of Epping at Woodford Church, Essex. He served this parish from 1641 until 1643. However, the events of the Civil War soon caught up with him and he was forced out of or sequestered from the parish for his religious views. Having private means he continued to preach in the eastern counties but operated mainly in the Epping area. Having been identified as a danger to Puritanism he was forced to keep a record of all sermons preached[iii]. This record starts with the words, 'On November 14th 1643 being Saturday the Sequestration of my liberty was made known to me. Every Sunday since, I have been in place of employment as followeth .....'. In this document he records all the sermons he preached and their sources from November 1643 until March 1645. Most of the Sundays he preached at Copthall (Copped Hall, Epping) but he was also present at several other venues including Coton and Crandon, Cambridgeshire and St Edward's Church, Cambridge. If he was not preaching on a Sunday he still had to record where he was and who preached the sermon.

Life for Thomas Holbech must have got considerably worse after the death of the king with the rule of the Puritans under Cromwell's Commonwealth. However he did find another parish to serve and the 1650s saw him as the priest at Chastleton on the Warwickshire, Gloucestershire border. However, his Royalist reputation followed him and he was ejected from the parish at the time of the rule of the Major-generals. Holbech wrote to his friend William Sancroft in March 1656 and commented that he had hoped to keep his royalist past secret but that, 'the malice of some made knowne soon enough to cut the throate of any such purpose'. He added that the local Major-general, Charles Fleetwood, might perhaps have shown him some favour, 'but he acts not at all in person and his commissioners I have no great fancy untoe'.

In 1660 with the restoration of the monarchy Holbech returned to his beloved Emmanuel College in Cambridge and also took up his post as the incumbent at Epping. The Restoration saw renewed life at Emmanuel with plans to build a new chapel. Holbech's wealth would be a great help for the college with a lecturer commenting that, 'the good Dr Holbech would be sure to lay £50 on the foundation stone'[iv]. Thomas Holbech also supported the building of the chapel during his lifetime by giving the lease of the Sempire Lands, 21 acres of arable and pasture to the south of Cambridge including Coe Fen Leys. Peterhouse College was the landlord but Holbech made over his lease to Emmanuel College on 17 March 1668. Rents were then obtained by sub-letting the property. The college thus received an income of £10 10s in return for an outlay of 19s 6d, six bushels of wheat and one quarter each of malt and oats. At the start of the chapel building the master of the college was Breton but he was succeeded by Thomas Holbech in 1676. He oversaw the project's completion which consisted of the glazing, wainscotting and paving in the very best black and white marble.

One of Thomas Holbech's innovations was a course of lectures in ecclesiastical history of no less than sixty lectures to run over four years at five per term. All students under the rank of MA were obliged to attend. This new course meant that Emmanuel College was perhaps the first English place of learning to provide specifically for the teaching of church history. Holbech had powerful friends who included William Sancroft, Archbishop of Canterbury. Pluralism was rife in the Church of England at this time and as well as his positions at Emmanuel and Epping, Holbech was Prebend of St. Paul's, London (1660-80) and Rector of St. Augustine, London. At Cambridge he was Vice-Chancellor during the period of 1677-78. He died in 1680. In his will he asked to be buried next to his wife, Anna in the parish church of Woodford in Essex. He planned to give £10 each to five poor widows of ministers and other gifts to the poor[v]. In his will he did not forget his beloved Emmanuel College and left it some fee-farm rents to the annual value of £50 13s 9d, £9 of which arose from lands called Highelman and Lowelman, which were part of the manors of Denny and Waterbeach near Cambridge. The rest of the income issued from the manor of Littleport. These rents, which were conveyed to the college on 18 April 1681, were to endow a catechist and ecclesiastical lecturer with annual stipends of £20 each. Of the remaining income half was to augment the stipend of the master and half was to be a contribution towards the repairs of the college. He left four pounds to his sister Anne Kittermaster of Coleshill and forty pounds to his nephew William of Westminster. William was the son of Thomas Holbech's brother, William. His other nephew was Thomas who was admitted to Emmanuel in April 1678. He later became rector of Holdenby, Northamptonshire but died young in 1690. Thomas Holbech also left twenty pounds for plate to his good friend William Sancroft, Archbishop of Canterbury and also forty shillings for Sancroft to buy a ring for his burial. There were also bequests to his nephews and nieces in the Cayley family. Mary Cayley received his rings with the escallops plus money and plate with the same coat of arms. Mary was the daughter of Barnaby Holbech, Thomas' brother. She had married Sir William Cayley of Brompton, Yorkshire in 1653. The Cayley family married into the Worsley family of Yorkshire and so with the marriage of Katharine Worsley to the Duke of Kent in 1961, Holbech genes became part of the royal family's make-up.

One interesting aspect of the life of Thomas Holbech of Birchley Hall was his interest in his family's history. The executor of his will was Ambrose Holbech of Mollington who inherited Thomas' papers which included pedigrees of the family.

[i] William Dugdale, *The Antiquities of Warwickshire*, Second Edition of William Thomas (1730), Volume 2, p. 63.

[ii] J. Venn & J.A.Venn, Alumni Cantabriginenses, Vol II (1922), p. 387.

[iii] Centre for Kentish Studies, Maidstone, Sackville Manuscripts, U269/Q13/6, The account by Thomas Holbech, vicar of Epping, Essex, 1645.

[iv] Sarah Bendall, Christopher Brooke & Patrick Collinson, *A History of Emmanuel College, Cambridge* (Woodbridge, 1999), pp. 274-275.

[v] Warwickshire Record Office, Holbeche Family Papers, CR/1680/669/12, Transcript of Will of Thomas Holbech.
Bodleian Library, Oxford, Tanner Collection, Vol. 155, p. 31.

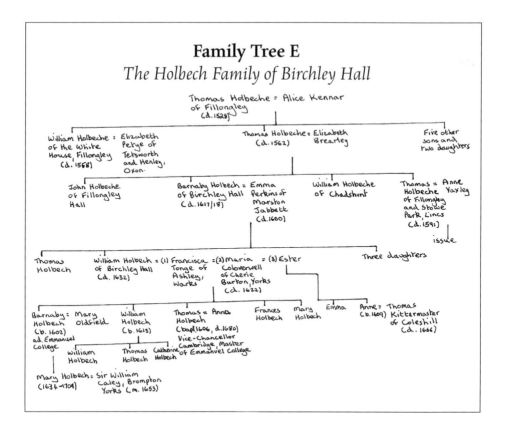

Plate 20 *Mary Holbech (1634-1709) of Birchley Hall.*
She married Sir William Cayley of Brompton, Yorkshire, in 1653.

Plate 21 Thomas Holbech (1606-1680) of Birchley Hall, Master of Emmanuel College, Cambridge.
(By permission of the Master and Fellows of Emmanuel College, Cambridge)

Chapter Four

The Holbech Family
of Stoneleigh

ONE IMPORTANT branch of the Holbech family was established at Corley and later at Stoneleigh in Warwickshire by the mid seventeenth century. Perhaps it was through this branch that the Barons Leigh became associated with the Holbech family through marriage.

The family members at Stoneleigh were often described as yeomen. Basil Holbech, who died in 1687 lived at Canley Hall. The inventory taken at his death lists the rooms in his house as a kitchen, hall, parlour, dairy house, kitchen chamber, green chamber, hall chamber, cheese chamber and a barn. His land consisted of 152 acres of enclosed land, 14 acres of winter corn, 33 acres of barley, peas and oats. His possessions were valued at £1,551 mainly because of a large amount of money listed in the inventory. His widow, Ann died in 1695 and occupied the same house and land.[i]

Basil's brother John also died in the same year. His inventory described him as a gentleman and he occupied Manor Farm in Stoneleigh. This house at one time had been occupied by the local landowners the Leigh family. Manor Farm was a large house which John Holbech occupied as a co-tenant with Francis Clayton. Holbech's part of the house consisted of his bedchamber, a chamber over the kitchen, a cheese chamber, chamber over the parlour, a parlour, a little room, hall, kitchen, brewhouse and dairy house. He held 73 acres of land and he was worth £100.[ii]

One member of this branch of the family pursued a career completely different to his landowning and farming relatives. This was Amilion Holbeche (Holbache) who died in Warwick in 1597. He was the owner of the Swan Inn in the High Street in Warwick. This was Warwick's most prestigious hostelry. It was a large house with two halls, six parlours and twenty chambers. This inn served the local community particularly when the court sessions were in progress. Several prominent families had rooms set aside for their particular needs. In the inventory compiled on Amilion's death some of the rooms have names such as Mr Verneys Chamber, Lady Digbies Chamber, Mr Ffishers Chamber and Sir Fowlks Chamber. His estate came to a considerable amount of money and property which he left mainly to his wife Elizabeth and his two daughters. The agricultural background of his family still is demonstrated by his ownership of 300 ewes.[iii] His will was witnessed by Barnaby Holbeche (Holbache) who he names as his uncle. He was a descendent of Clement Holbeche of Fillongley. Barnaby Holbeche held the position of Bailiff of Warwick in 1594 and 1606. The Bailiff of Warwick at that time was the position we would now call mayor. These members of the Holbeche family demonstrate important contributions made to the government and development of Warwick during the late sixteenth century. However these lines of the family were extinct by the mid seventeenth century.

---

[i]   N.W. Alcock, *People at Home, Living in a Warwickshire Village, 1500-1800* (Chichester, 1993), pp. 91-92.

[ii] N.W. Alcock (1993), p. 74.

[iii] *The Warwickshire Antiquarian Magazine*, Edited By John Fetherston, Parts I to VIII, 1859-1877 pp. 198-209.

Family Tree F
The Holbechs of Corley and Stoneleigh

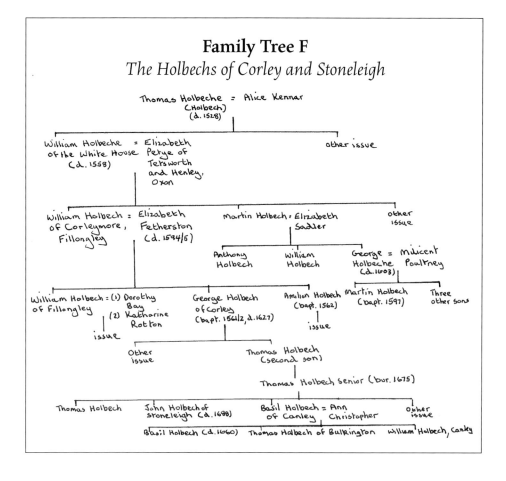

Thomas Holbeche = Alice Kennar
(Holbech)
(d. 1528)

William Holbeche = Elizabeth Petye of Tetsworth and Henley, Oxon
of the White House
(d. 1558)

other issue

William Holbech = Elizabeth Fetherston (d. 1594/5)
of Corleymore, Fillongley

Martin Holbech = Elizabeth Sadler

other issue

Anthony Holbech

William Holbech

George = Milicent Poultney
Holbeche (d. 1603)

William Holbech = (1) Dorothy Bay (2) Katharine Rotton
of Fillongley

George Holbech of Corley (bapt. 1561/2, d. 1627)

Amulion Holbech (bapt. 1562)

Martin Holbech (bapt. 1597)

Three other sons

issue

issue

Other issue

Thomas Holbech (second son)

Thomas Holbech Senior (bur. 1675)

Thomas Holbech

John Holbech of Stoneleigh (d. 1698)

Basil Holbech = Ann Christopher
of Canley

other issue

Basil Holbech (d. 1660)

Thomas Holbech of Bulkington

William Holbech, Canley

43

Chapter Five

The Holbech Family
of Solihull

ANOTHER IMPORTANT branch of the Holbech family became
established at Solihull in Warwickshire. The first link with this area to the
Holbech family came with membership of the Guild of Knowle. Knowle is a
village on the edge of Solihull and in medieval times was host to an important
guild. The objects of this guild was religious worship with aid in time of need to
members in sickness, old age, poverty and during loss. Guilds also regularly held
social and business meetings with periodical feasts. Other important aspects of
guild membership was to encourage charity and useful living. Members were
admitted on payment of entrance fees and had to take oaths to observe the rules
of the guild. Further expenses were supported by donations and annual
subscriptions. There was a chapel at Knowle in the thirteenth century but it
appears to have been refounded and revived later by Walter Cook towards the end
of the reign of Richard II. Construction of the church was so far advanced by 1399
that services could be held there. During the reign of Henry IV Walter Cook and
his father, Adam were given permission to establish a chantry of one or two priests
to celebrate divine service perpetually at Knowle. In the next year the same Walter
Cook granted to the monks of Westminster and their successors, the advowson
and patronage of the chantry. In 1412 Walter Cook founded, with six other men,
the Guild of St Anne at Knowle and at its most popular it had over 3,000
members. The guild for the most part seems to have been composed of the

ordinary people of Warwickshire. The parishes west of Knowle furnished more members than those parishes to the east. At the commencement of the sixteenth centuries more influential people were members. These included the Marquis of Dorset, the Earl of Kent, the Abbots of Evesham, Pershore and Bordesley. Sir Richard Empson and his wife were also members during this period. Membership of the Guild of Knowle allowed association with a group of people who could exchange knowledge and opportunities with fellow guild members.

As early as 1460 the Guild of Knowle had Holbech members, they were John Holbeche and his wife Alice.[i] In 1483 Thomas Holbeche and his wife Alice were members.[ii] In 1511 the membership of the guild included Richard Holbech and his wife, and they are described as of Solihull.[iii] In the following year the membership of the guild included John and Thomas Holbech along with his wife Elizabeth.[iv] This renewed interest in the guild by the Holbech family could be associated with the fact that their near neighbours and relatives from Fillongley, the Brearley family were members and officers of the guild. In fact John Brearley of Fillongley was master of the guild in 1512. Thomas Holbech's wife Elizabeth was the daughter of Richard Brearley. John Holbech was of Fillongley Hall and had married Elizabeth, the widow of John Dabridgecourt of Solihull. Richard was the son of Thomas Holbech and seems to have established himself at Solihull by 1511. It must have been through membership of the Guild of Knowle that he realised that opportunities existed in the Solihull area for land ownership and development and so moved from Fillongley.

Richard Holbech had settled at Bentley Heath, Solihull by 1511 and by 1520 was occupying Widney Manor. He married Anne Smallbrooke of Yardley. As usual service to the church was to the fore and he was a churchwarden in 1532 and in 1549.[v] He died in 1551. He had three sons and two daughters. Edward, described as a yeoman was a churchwarden at Solihull. He died unmarried in 1605. Richard's eldest son was Barnaby who also served as churchwarden in 1562. He was married in 1549 to Dorothy Fetherston and died in 1586. His son, Thomas succeeded as tenant of Widney Manor. He was later granted or purchased the manor on the attainder of John Somerville, the owner, in 1592. He married Isabella Holmes of Yardley. He had three sons and five daughters and he died in 1634/35. His contribution to community affairs was to hold the post of Surveyor of Highways.

His eldest daughter Elizabeth married her cousin William Holbeche of Pinfold House, Fillongley. A large mural tablet was set up in the Chapel of St Katherine within the church of St Alphege, Solihull commemorating Elizabeth. This was done according to the will of her nephew William Holbech. Her second brother was Barnaby who was baptised in December 1597. He married Marie Gore of Ullesthorpe. Leicestershire. The Gore family is a prime example of the type of position the Holbech family would have occupied within Solihull society. The Gore family occupied a similar position in Leicestershire. They were descended from the Gores of Wiltshire and were one of only two families living in the neighbourhood of Lutterworth who bore arms. Thomas Gore became the lord of the manor of Ullesthorpe and had large holdings of land and pasture. At Bittesby in 1599 Thomas Gore had 247 sheep worth seventeen shillings each and four bullocks or steers worth £3 each. This type of family was not connected so much with the foremost gentry as with the leading yeomanry in the area. However, the Holbech family and the Gores were examples of the forerunners of the new local gentry of the next century. Barnaby Holbech held the post of Parish Bailiff of Solihull, a position harking back to the original family roots at Fillongley. However, even parish officers could overstep the mark for in 1638 he was indicted at the Quarter Sessions for digging and making a marl pit near the highway in Solihull. This was the main road from Warwick to Birmingham and for this offence he received a fine.[vi] He died in 1645 and was succeeded by his son Thomas. He was born in 1632 and married Elizabeth Clapham of Winnal Hall, Warwickshire. He followed his father as Parish Bailiff and Feoffee and later died in 1712. These members of the Solihull branch of the family were often described as yeomen. They owned land, farmed and obtained the position of members of the lesser gentry. Thomas Holbech seems to have been successful enough to invest a considerable sum in building Touchwood Hall in Solihull. However, it was to be the children of Thomas Holbech (1632-1712) who were to lift the family into the higher levels of society as well as amassing large fortunes.

Thomas Holbech's eldest son was also called Thomas. He seems to have had a deep interest in his family's history. He was educated at Trinity College, Oxford where he was awarded a BA in 1684. He compiled a genealogical tree of the Meriden branch of the family and produced a work entitled *A Handbook on*

Heraldry which chiefly referred to his own line. Both works must have existed only in manuscript form and are now not extant. Thomas Holbech BA died in around 1692 approximately aged thirty. It was his researches that contributed to the family history contained on the large mural tablet that was erected in St Katherine's chapel at the parish church of St Alphege, Solihull. This tablet was erected in 1726. However, as with many family pedigrees there is certainly one personality mentioned that appears to have been co-opted into the family. Although most of the family history on the mural tablet is correct there is an interloper present. This is Henry Holbech who in the sixteenth century is praised for compiling the prayers then in use in the church of England and who also was Bishop of Lincoln. In fact, his real name was de Randes and he changed his name to Holbech as he came from Holbeach in Lincolnshire. In some of the ancient family pedigrees the family line starts with Oliver de Randes Holbech, a move designed to incorporate Henry Holbech into the family. Many of the existing pedigrees were later altered, probably in the nineteenth century, to excise the name de Randes from prominence and so correctly name the earliest traced member of the family as plain Oliver Holbech.

With the death of Thomas Holbech in 1692 the head of the family became Anthony Holbech, his brother, who was born in 1662. However, at this period he was spending little time in Solihull. As with many members of the Holbech family, both in Fillongley and Solihull, he had been sent away to learn a trade. In 1678 Anthony Holbech was apprenticed to Thomas Harwell in London to learn the art of distilling.[vii] The Holbech family had probably heard from relatives of the opportunities that existed in this developing industry. A distant relative, Simon Holbech of Newton, Leicester had been apprenticed in the distilling trade in the previous year and another relative Martin Brearley of Fillongley was an apprenticed distiller from 1670/71. Anthony Holbech's apprenticeship was successful and he soon set himself up in business and took on his own apprentices. In 1687 Anthony Holbech took Edward Tolly as an apprentice and in 1691/92 he took his own brother, Samuel as an apprentice.[viii] There seems to have been some subterfuge in this move as in the records of the Worshipful Company of Distillers Samuel's father is named as William Holbech not as Thomas. The taking of a very close relative as an apprentice would have probably been frowned on so this strategy was used by the Holbech brothers to bring respectability to the arrangement. Anthony and Samuel Holbech seem to have spent many years as distillers in the city of London. At least four of Anthony Holbech's children were born in London, namely, Elizabeth (1701), Thomas (1704), Anthony (1706) and Elizabeth (1708). All were christened in the connected London parishes of St Nicholas Cole Abbey and St Nicholas Olave. The church of St Nicholas Olave had been burned down in the Great Fire of 1666 and had not been rebuilt. The parish had been united with that of St Nicholas Cole Abbey. This was the first city church built by Wren after the Great Fire. During its history this church had maintained a close link with fishmongers and in medieval times there was a fish market near the church. From the number of fishmongers buried there during the sixteenth century, it would appear to have maintained a close association with the fish trade which began in the reign of Richard I. It was probably here that Samuel Holbech met his wife for he married Anne Walton, the daughter of the Royal Fishmonger.

The Holbech brothers could not have set up their distillery at a more advantageous time. In 1689 the throne was offered to Mary and her Dutch husband William. James II escaped to France and William and Mary occupied the throne. France was now Britain's enemy and all trade with the country ceased. William and his allies brought with them the habit of gin drinking and with brandy being unobtainable from the continent it produced the impetus for the growth of the distilling industry in England. A distilling industry had existed before this time but it was small and used inferior grain. Suddenly it was patriotic to drink gin and it provided a new market for the sale of corn and rye. Gin drinking tended to be concentrated in cities where the distillers operated. There were two types of distillery. There were the malt distillers who produced pure spirits. These were large scale enterprises and in Greater London they were represented by the Company of Distillers. The second stage of production was carried out by compound distillers who flavoured the raw spirits with a variety of additives such as juniper berries. The compound distillers were both numerous and small-scale.[ix] The Holbech brothers were involved in malt distilling in which large fortunes could be made through the boom in gin drinking. Members of the Distilling Company were to be counted amongst the most wealthy and powerful manufacturing interests in England.[x] Anthony Holbech appears to have been one of these industrialists. He must have risen to the top of his profession for during 1715-1717 he was a member of the Court of the Worshipful Company of Distillers and in July 1717 he was listed as a Warden of the Distillers' Company. This was followed by his elevation to the post of Master of the Worshipful Company of Distillers during the period October 1718 until the end of 1719. Anthony Holbech continued to attend the Court and his last appearance seems to have been in October 1730.[xi] By 1720 when he was 58 he appears to have been in semi-retirement for in that year he was appointed as churchwarden at the parish church of Solihull.

If Anthony Holbech's trade was to bring him a fortune then so did his marriage. In 1701 he married Jane the daughter of John Parsons. John Parsons was born in 1643 and entered the trade of brewing as his father owned the Red Lion Brewery positioned just east of the Tower of London. The speciality of this brewery became a beer with a high alcoholic content. It was a stout made from fermented malt, with very little, if any, hops and it possessed a separate legal definition in the Customs and Excise Act. It received a tribute from Oliver Goldsmith who called it 'Parsons Black Champagne'.

The Parsons family were very well connected within the trading life of the City of London and with its governance. Parsons' mother was the daughter of Humphrey Beane who was Master of the Cordwainers' Company and was an alderman in London. He was also a great trading merchant who owned land in Surrey and Wales. He had a great interest in the whale fisheries off Greenland and was also a farmer of the Hearth Tax. In the late seventeenth and early eighteenth centuries Government taxes were not collected directly but farmed out to the highest bidder as a profit making concern. John Parsons had a similar trading background to his father-in-law. He was a London alderman and master of the Brewers' Company in 1687 and in that year he was knighted. He had total control of the Red Lion Brewery from 1677 and was a Freeman of the City of London. In 1681 John Parsons bought Reigate Priory and its estate in Surrey. He was an MP for Reigate from 1685 until 1715. Parsons business empire included his role as Commissioner for Victualling the Navy. He was also one of the farmers who collected the Excise Tax which would have included the levy on distillers.[xii]

This is how he would have met Anthony Holbech which would lead Holbech to marry his daughter. The dowry for this marriage would have greatly increased the Holbech family's finances. Sir John Parsons had a great ambition which he found difficult to attain. He wanted to be Lord Mayor of London. When candidates were nominated for the post there was a distinct hierarchy for choosing the mayor. Parsons was in the Brewers' Company which was fourteenth in the pecking order. Parsons realised that to obtain his ambition he must try to join a different city company. Anthony Holbech married Jane Parsons in 1701 and soon it was the Holbech brothers who were to manipulate the change of company for Parsons. Parsons joined the Fishmongers' Company which was fourth in precedence. Samuel Holbech was married to the daughter of the Royal Fishmonger and this is how his membership of the new company was engineered. In 1703 John Parsons was elected as Lord Mayor of London.[xiii] He is remembered chiefly for his generosity for he gave up many of his official fees to be put towards the payment of the city's debts and for the relief of the poor and orphans. In Reigate Sir John Parsons celebrated his year in high office by presenting to the parish church a fine brass candelabrum with two tiers of eight branches for candles, a dove finial and coloured scrolling. This was dated 1704. Anthony Holbech followed his father-in-law's lead for he presented St Alphege's Church in Solihull with a single tier candelabrum of eight candles. This is dated 1706 and is inscribed with Anthony's name and the name of his father, Thomas.

In retirement Anthony Holbech seems to have devoted his life to local church and parish matters in Solihull. He was elected as churchwarden in 1720.[xiv] Several of his children had died at an early age and to add to his sadness a serious rift occurred with his surviving son, Clapham Holbech. The story of this rift is that Clapham scaled the outside of the spire of Solihull Church for a wager. When he descended he was so mercilessly thrashed by his father that he ran away from home and went abroad. As well as running away he also received the nickname of 'The Steeple Flyer'. Clapham Holbech had received a legal training for in 1731 he was admitted to the Inner Temple. Anthony Holbech died in 1738 but disaster soon followed for Clapham died in the following year before he could return to England. Legal proceedings seem to have taken place for Anthony's cousins who lived in Alvechurch later put in a claim on the estate as they were the only male heirs. This seems to have rumbled on for a considerable time until the case was finally thrown out in 1830.[xv] Several generations after the death of Anthony Holbech, the Alvechurch branch of the family would claim that the Short family had benefited by £70,000 from the estate.[xvi] This indicates the size of the fortune that Anthony and his brother Samuel had gathered by their endeavours in London. The final proceedings of the court case in 1830 gives some details about the fate of Clapham Holbech. This does seem to indicate a serious rift within the family. When he died he was a lowly clerk to the Company of Merchants Trading to Africa. He met his death in about 1739 at the Georgetown Factory on the River Gambia in Africa. Here he drowned in the river, possibly having been trapped in quicksand.

After the death of Anthony Holbech the female members of his family were given much support by John Holbech (1670-1753) who was Anthony's brother. He, too had made his mark in London society but in a completely different sphere. Official documents tell the story of his rise for, 'About the latter end of King James the Second's reign, admitted first Clerk in the Treasury of the Great Chamber's Office, in which office, for his diligent and faithful discharge of his duty, was afterwards made Deputy-Treasurer. And in some part of the reign of Her Late Majesty Queen Anne of pious memory, solely discharged the Office of Treasurer of the Great-Chamber. And was likewise sworn and admitted into the accompting office, in which station, as well as Deputy-Treasurer of the Great-Chamber, and likewise one of His Majesty's Justices of the Peace for the County of Warwick. He now continues under the auspicious Reign of His Most Excellent Majesty King George.' The document later added that he, 'Had the honour of being a domestick continually in the service of five crowned heads of Great Britain from the year 1688 and is at this time a servant to his present Majesty King George II in his Royal Household, 1748'.[xvii] He married Elizabeth, the daughter and heiress of John Day of Stogursey in Somerset. They had one son, Day Holbech (1710-1764). He served as a page to Queen Anne and later held other royal posts including the post of Watering the King's Highway. When he died he left his Somerset property to his Day relatives in that county. He left some property in London and Solihull to his Holbech relatives in Solihull as well as leaving them his domestic goods, plate and jewels.[xviii]

With the death of Anthony Holbech the male line continued through his cousins at Alvechurch in Worcestershire. Anthony's uncle, Barnaby Holbeche had married Elizabeth the daughter of William Hollington, the Rector of Alvechurch. He appears to have settled at Alvechurch in about 1674/75 and he and his descendants consistently spelt his surname name with the 'e'. William Hollington was a doctor of divinity and at one time Rector of Alvechurch from 1641. He was a staunch royalist and acted as one of the chaplains to both Charles I and Charles II. His Royalist views were not in sympathy with many of his parishioners. Many of the clergy were accused of all sorts of misdemeanours when the parishioners wanted a priest more in favour of Parliament's views of religion. In the Quarter Sessions in 1643 the Constable of Alvechurch complained that Hollington was a frequenter of alehouses, kept riotous and idle company causing drunkenness by forcing others to drink whole cups, of incontinence with neighbours' wives, of favouring papists, of being a cursor and a liar. It seems that the Sessions took no action at this time realising that these accusations were part of a campaign to have him ejected. Although this was resisted, by 1646 the Civil War was going badly for the king and Hollington was ejected from his parish. He was accused of stating that, 'Papists in Ireland were honester men than any Protestants. He hindered the parishoners from taking protestation, and was party to the forcible carrying off of a widow's daughter aged 14 to marry a rude boy of idle behavior'.[xix] He later became the rector of Long Marston in Gloucestershire, then Vicar of Wichenford in Worcestershire and then rector of Exhall before returning to Alvechurch as the incumbent with the restoration of Charles II.

The Holbeche family in Alvechurch continued to lease and farm land. In the nineteenth century they were mainly based at Seecham Farm, later called Seecham Manor Farm. Here they farmed 137 acres and occupied a pretty half-timbered farm house. This is a T-plan timber-framed house comprising a two-bay hall range and passage dated to 1474 and a four bay cross-wing dated to 1595. The name Seecham was first used in the early nineteenth century and replaced the building's earlier name of Rowney Green House. In the sixteenth century the freehold land at Rowney Green was owned by the Milward family. In the 1680s the estate was bought by Richard Booth who was a London grocer who let out the house and lands to tenant farmers. In 1817 the house and land was purchased by

James Luckcock who was a Birmingham buckle and button maker. He made alterations to the house but never came to live there. Luckcock leased the property firstly to John Holbeche and then to his son Johnathan.[xx] By the end of the nineteenth century several members of the Holbeche family had left Alvechurch and returned to Solihull.

In Solihull after the death of Anthony Holbech and his wife Jane, the estate was inherited mainly by his daughter Mary. She married the Rev. Richard Mashiter who was headmaster of Solihull Grammar School. They had three children but only the daughter Jane Mashiter (1745-1831) married. She married John Short and they had seven children. One of these was Mary Short (1775-1883) who married the Rev. Boughey William Dolling (1782-1853). Dolling was to later move to Ireland and much of the Holbech silver and many of the family portraits were moved to that location. Other family portraits descended through Jane Short who married John Edwards and then through descent in the Couchman family.

The Holbech descendants through the Dolling family show the same characteristics of the main family, namely devotion to the church and charity and a deep interest in their family history. The Dolling family were originally from France and were members of a Huguenot group that fled to Britain to escape persecution. The Dolling family numbered several clergymen in their line. Boughey William Dolling attained a fellowship at Exeter College, Oxford and later became the incumbent at Magheralin, County Down where he set up home with his wife, Mary Short. While at Magheralin Dolling built a new church which was consecrated in 1845. Dolling's eldest son was named Robert Holbeche Dolling (1809-1878). He was trained in law and was a D.L. and barrister. After his education he became the agent for the estates of Lord Rossmore. In 1859 he was appointed agent for the important estates of the Mercers' Company in Northern Ireland and moved with his family to the Manor House, Kilrea, County Derry. He was described as, 'A most warm-hearted, genial man, full of wit and humour, without one single touch of malice, abounding in loving kindness to his fellow creatures'. R.H. Dolling was deeply religious with an interest in the Protestant Evangelical school. However, he was a man of very strong prejudices. The Roman Catholic Church and the High Church party in England were objects of his antipathy. In 1865 Robert Holbeche Dolling was appointed High Sheriff for Londonderry.

With the rather entrenched Protestant views adopted by R.H. Dolling it is surprising that his eldest son grew up to adhere to a completely different code of the Christian religion. He was Robert William Radclyffe Dolling (1851-1902) who was known as Father Dolling. He was educated at Harrow School and Trinity College, Cambridge. He entered the Church of England and became a parish priest. He was soon attracted to the High Church movement, which were completely opposite to his father's idea of the Christian religion. Dolling was soon taking his ministry to difficult areas and developed into a strong adherent to Anglo-Catholicism. He was a charismatic preacher and soon was touring Britain preaching. He was appointed to a mission at Landport, Portsmouth which in 1885 was one of the most run down and difficult parts of the city with its proximity to the Naval Docks. Dolling's evangelical and social work at Landport made him famous and he managed to raise enough money to build a new church. This was St Agatha's Church, Landport. Dolling had been impressed by the basilica churches of northern Italy with their rich decorative schemes and open plans. This allowed the congregation to see and hear the actions of the priest at the altar which was a far cry from the Gothic churches of Victorian England. Just as the church was nearing completion Dolling became embroiled in an argument with the church authorities. He wanted three altars in the church but this was too much for the Church of England. So after ten years in the post Dolling resigned and moved to another parish. This too was in a difficult area for he moved to Poplar in the East End of London. Dolling recorded his experiences at Portsmouth in a book entitled, *Ten Years In A Portsmouth Slum*. Dolling continued his evangelical work in London and was a sought after speaker for missionary work around Britain. He died in May 1902.[xxi] His church at Landport survived the bombing of the Second World War. However, enemy action cleared away the housing from around St Agatha's. The church was declared redundant and then used by the Royal Navy Dockyard as a storehouse. Plans were drawn up for the redevelopment of the area in the 1970s which would have meant the demolition of the church. The church was saved but several times was threatened with demolition in later years. In 1987 St Agatha's was given Listed Building status. A trust was formed to look after the building and major restoration of the fabric took place. Anglo-Catholic services are now once again held at St Agatha's.

Just before the outbreak of the First World War a member of the Holbech family from Farnborough Hall travelled to Belfast to attend a religious conference. He was taken to the Ulster Club for a meal and entertainment by the organiser. Not being a member he had to sign the visitors' book. This member of the family was later approached by a man who had seen his name in the visitors' book. He told the visitor that they must be related as he was descended from the Holbech family and had many articles in his possession of Holbech interest. His name was Boughey William Dolling Montgomery and he was Father Dolling's cousin. His Holbech possessions included no less than seven portraits of members of the family. He had these portraits photographed and sent the prints to Farnborough Hall. However, the photographs were not of that branch of the family but of the Solihull Holbech line. These photographs were later passed on to another Holbeche family member and are still preserved in the family. B.W.D. Montgomery lived at Mount Lyons, Antrim Road, Belfast and died unmarried in November 1917. He was a director of the Belfast firm of John Preston & Co. When he died he left a large estate and the charitable leanings of the Holbech family seem to be in the fore again. By his will dated, September 1917 he left bequests to the Masonic Lodge No 10 at 16 Alfred Street, Belfast, Masonic Orphan Boys' School, Dublin, Masonic Orphan Girls' School, Dublin, Victoria Jubilee Masonic Annuity Fund, Belfast Masonic Widows' Fund, Belfast Masonic Charities Fund, Protestant Orphans' Society for the counties of Antrim and Down, the Protestant Orange Widows' Fund and the Church of Ireland. His gifts to the masons were recognised and recorded for one of the Belfast groups meets as the Boughey William Dolling Montgomery Lodge. Exhaustive searches have been made to try to locate the whereabouts of the Holbech paintings and other artefacts that were in the ownership of B.W.D. Montgomery but these researches have drawn a blank. I can only think that these Holbech mementoes were destroyed perhaps during the Second World War when Belfast was heavily bombed. Perhaps someone in the future will be able to tell us the full story of these Irish Holbech portraits.

---

[i] *The Register of the Guild of Knowle*, Edited by W.B. Bickley (Walsall 1894), p. 33.
[ii] *The Register of the Guild of Knowle*, p. 88.
[iii] *The Register of the Guild of Knowle*, p. 204.
[iv] *The Register of the Guild of Knowle*, pp. 206-207

v   Robert Pemberton, *Solihull and its Church* (Exeter, 1905), p. 140.

vi   *Warwick County Records, Vol. IV, Quarter Sessions Order Book, Easter 1657 to Epiphany 1669*, Edited by S.C. Ratcliffe & H.C. Johnson (Warwick 1938), p. 49.

vii   Cliff Webb, *London Apprentices, Vol. 11, Distillers' Company 1659-1811* (London 1997), p. 15.

viii Cliff Webb, *London Apprentices, Vol 11, Distillers' Company 1659-1811*, p. 29 & p. 15.

ix   Jessica Warner, *Craze, Gin and Debauchery in an Age of Reason* (2003), p.27

x   Michael Berlin, *The Worshipful Company of Distillers, A Short History* (Chichester, 1996), p. 45.

xi   Guildhall Library, London, Ms 6207/1, Minutes of the Worshipful Company of Distillers.

xii   J.R. Woodhead, *The Rulers of London 1660-1689* (1965), pp. 124-134.

xiii Audrey Ward, *Discovering Reigate Priory* (Reigate, 1998) pp. 30-41.

xiv Robert Pemberton, *Solihull and its Church*, p. 143.

xv   Birmingham Reference Library, Crowder & Smallwood Collection, Ms3083/Acc1907-002/205386, Affidavit, signed by Jane Short, wife of John Short, surgeon concerning the Holbeche family, 5 April 1830.

xvi Warwickshire Record Office, Holbeche Family Papers, CR 1680/709, R.H. Holbeche to Mr Heaton, 25 September 1978.

xvii Warwickshire Record Office, Holbeche Family Papers, 1680/629, File 4.

xviii Warwickshire Record Office, Holbeche Family Papers, 1680/670, Transcript of will of Day Holbech, proved January 27 1764.

xix Warwick Record Office, Holbeche Family Papers, 1680/625, p. 339.

xx   W. Eileen Davies, *Beauchamps* (Studley, 1988), pp. 83-86.

xxi Rev. C.E. Osborne, *Life of Father Dolling* (1903).

Family Tree G
The Holbech Family of Solihull

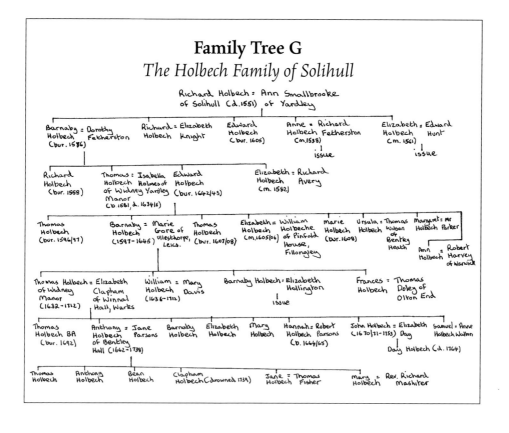

Richard Holbech = Ann Smallbrooke
of Solihull (d.1551) of Yardley

Barnaby = Dorothy Holbech Fetherston (bur. 1586)

Richard = Elizabeth Holbech Knight

Edward Holbech (bur. 1605)

Anne = Richard Holbech Fetherston (m.1538)
issue

Elizabeth = Edward Holbech Hunt (m. 1561)
issue

Richard Holbech (bor. 1558)

Thomas = Isabella Holbech Holmes of Widney Yardley Manor (b.1581, d.1634|5)

Edward Holbech (bur. 1642/43)

Elizabeth = Richard Holbech Avery (m. 1582)

Thomas Holbech (bur. 1596/97)

Barnaby = Marie Holbech Gore of (1597-1645) Ullesthorpe, Leics.

Thomas Holbech (bur. 1607/08)

Elizabeth = William Holbech Holbeche (m.1605/06) of Pinfold House, Fillongley

Marie Holbech

Ursula = Thomas Holbech Wilson of Bentley Heath

Margaret = Mr Holbech Parker

Ann = Robert Holbech Harvey of Warwick

Thomas Holbech = Elizabeth of Widney Clapham Manor of Winnal (1632-1712) Hall, Warks

William = Mary Holbech Davis (1636-1712)

Barnaby Holbech = Elizabeth Hollington
issue

Frances = Thomas Holbech Doley of Olton End

Thomas Holbech BA (bur. 1692)

Anthony = Jane Holbech Parsons of Bentley Hall (1662-1738)

Barnaby Holbech

Elizabeth Holbech

Mary Holbech

Hannah = Robert Holbech Parsons (b. 1664/65)

John Holbech = Elizabeth (1670/71-1753) Day

Samuel = Anne Holbech Walton (d. 1764)

Day Holbech (d. 1764)

Thomas Holbech

Anthony Holbech

Bean Holbech

Clapham Holbech (drowned 1739)

Jane = Thomas Holbech Fisher

Mary = Rev. Richard Holbech Mashiter

Family Tree H
The Hollington Family of Alvechurch

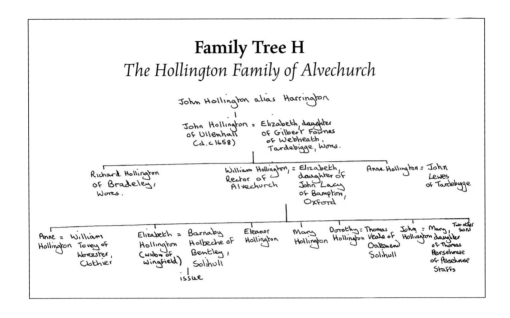

John Hollington alias Harrington

John Hollington = Elizabeth, daughter
of Ullenhall   of Gilbert Fownes
(d. c 1658)   of Webheath,
                Tardebigge, Worcs.

Richard Hollington
of Bradeley,
Worcs.

William Hollington, = Elizabeth,
Rector of   daughter of
Alvechurch   John Lacy
                       of Bampton,
                       Oxford

Anne Hollington = John
                  Lewes
                  of Tardebigge

Anne = William
Hollington Tovey of
         Worcester,
         Clothier

Elizabeth = Barnaby
Hollington Holbeche of
(widow of   Bentley,
Wingfield) Solihull
            issue

Eleanor
Hollington

Mary
Hollington

Dorothy = Thomas
Hollington Veale of
           Oakenend
           Solihull

John = Mary,
Hollington daughter
           of Thomas
           Persehouse
           of Persehouse
           Staffs

Two other
sons

Family Tree I
The Holbeches of Alvechurch

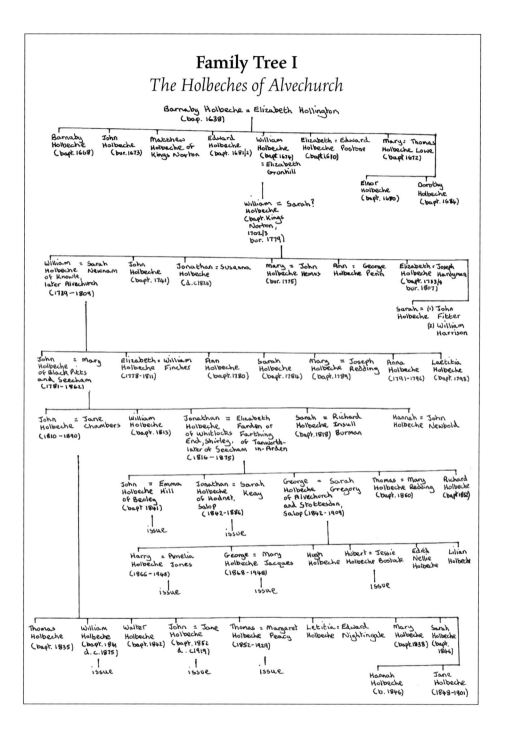

Family Tree J

The Dolling and Montgomery Descent from the Holbech Family

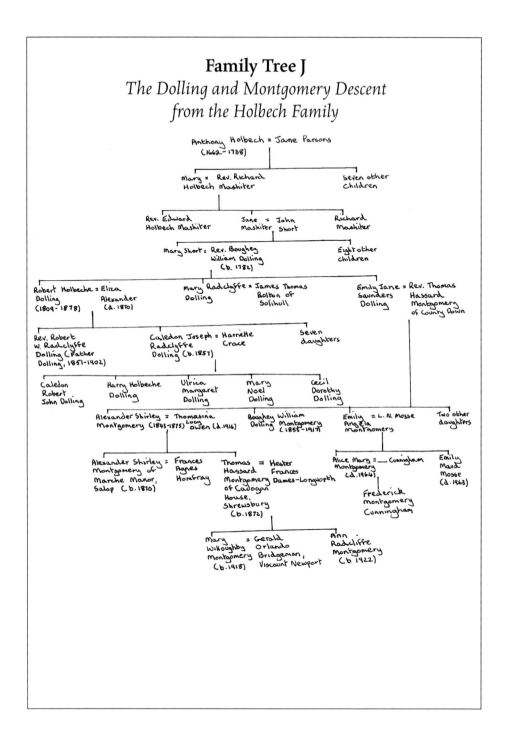

Plate 22 The Church of St John the Baptist, St Lawrence and St Anne, Knowle.

Plate 23 The Guild House beside the church at Knowle. It was the attractions of membership of the Guild of Knowle that brought the Holbeche family to the Solihull area.

Plate 24 Thomas Holbech (d. 1692), one of the seventeenth century historians of the family.

Plate 25 Anthony Holbech of Bentley Hall (1662-1738). It was his career as a distiller in London that renewed the fortunes of the family.

Plate 26 Jane Holbech, wife of Anthony and daughter of Sir John Parsons.

Plate 27 The arms of Anthony Holbech taken from an eighteenth century pedigree roll produced for the family. Oxidation has turned the green background colours to blue.

Plate 28 The church of St Nicholas Cole Abbey, London. This was the church in London attended by Anthony Holbech and his family. His children were christened here and the church is famous as being the first church built by Wren in London after the Great Fire.

Plate 29 Reigate Priory, the home of the Parsons family in the eighteenth century.

Oliver of Hol:
bech in the County of Lin
coln, married and had
issue.

Plate 30 A rather fanciful depiction of Oliver Holbech which starts the eighteenth century pedigree roll of the family. The gap in the inscription shows where the name de Randes has later been removed.

Plate 31 Thomas Holbech (1632-1712), eldest son
of Barnaby Holbech.

Plate 32 Elizabeth Holbech, wife of Thomas
Holbech, daughter of Luke Clapham of Winnal
Hall, near Coventry.

Plate 33 John Holbech of Whitehall, London
(1670-1753).

Plate 34 Elizabeth, wife of John Holbech and
daughter of John Day of Somerset.

Plate 35 *The arms of John Holbech from the eighteenth century pedigree roll.*

Plate 36 *Clapham Holbech (d.1739), son of Anthony Holbech and nicknamed 'The Steeple Flyer'.*

Plate 37 *Mary Mashiter, daughter of Anthony Holbech and wife of Dr Richard Mashiter, the headmaster of Solihull Grammar School.*

Plate 38 *Day Holbech (1710-1764), son of John and Elizabeth Holbech. He is dressed as a page to Queen Anne.*

Plate 39 *The parish church of St Alphege, Solihull.*

Plate 40 The eight branch candelabrum given to St Alphege's Church, Solihull by Anthony Holbech in 1706.

Plate 41 The Holbech monument in St Katherine's Chapel in the parish church of St Alphege, Solihull.

Plate 42 A close up of the inscriptions and heraldry on the Holbech Monument in the parish church, Solihull.

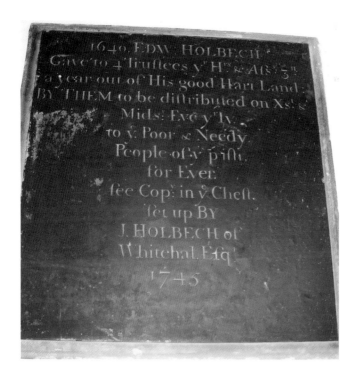

Plate 43 A memorial tablet in St Katherine's Chapel set up by John Holbech of Whitehall commemorating a charitable gift by Edward Holbech.

Plate 44 The second Holbech tablet set up by John Holbech in St Katherine's Chapel.

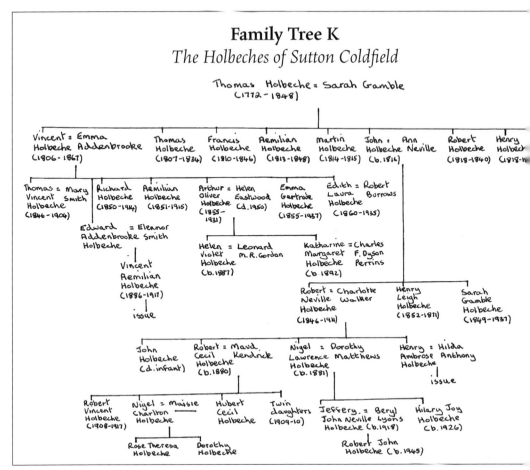

Family Tree K
The Holbeches of Sutton Coldfield

Thomas Holbeche = Sarah Gamble
(1772-1848)

Vincent = Emma
Holbeche Addenbrooke
(1806-1867)

Thomas
Holbeche
(1807-1834)

Francis
Holbeche
(1810-1846)

Aemilian
Holbeche
(1813-1848)

Martin
Holbeche
(1814-1815)

John = Ann
Holbeche Neville
(b.1816)

Robert
Holbeche
(1818-1840)

Henry
Holbeche
(1818-1...)

Thomas = Mary
Vincent Smith
Holbeche
(1846-1904)

Richard
Holbeche
(1850-1944)

Aemilian
Holbeche
(1851-1915)

Arthur = Helen
Oliver Eastwood
Holbeche (d.1950)
(1855-
1931)

Emma
Gertrude
Holbeche
(1855-1937)

Edith = Robert
Laura Burrows
Holbeche
(1860-1935)

Edward = Eleanor
Addenbrooke Smith
Holbeche

Helen = Leonard
Violet M.R.Gordon
Holbeche
(b.1887)

Katharine = Charles
Margaret F.Dyson
Holbeche Perrins
(b.1892)

Vincent
Aemilian
Holbeche
(1886-1917)

Robert = Charlotte
Neville Walker
Holbeche
(1846-1911)

Henry
Leigh
Holbeche
(1852-1871)

Sarah
Gamble
Holbeche
(1849-1937)

issue

John
Holbeche
(d.infant)

Robert = Maud
Cecil Kendrick
Holbeche
(b.1880)

Nigel = Dorothy
Lawrence Matthews
Holbeche
(b.1881)

Henry = Hilda
Ambrose Anthony
Holbeche

issue

Robert
Vincent
Holbeche
(1908-1917)

Nigel = Maisie
Charlton
Holbeche

Hubert
Cecil
Holbeche

Twin
daughters
(1909-10)

Jeffery = Beryl
John Neville Lyons
Holbeche (b.1918)

Hilary Joy
Holbeche
(b.1926)

Rose Theresa
Holbeche

Dorothy
Holbeche

Robert John
Holbeche (b.1945)

*Plate 45 The Rev. Robert W.
Radclyffe Dolling (1851-1902).*

...h	Mary	Elizabeth	Jane	Catharine	Helen	Frances
...eche	Holbeche	Holbeche	Holbeche	Holbeche	Holbeche	Holbeche
(...03-1882)	(1805-1884)	(1809-1858)	(1812-1891)	(1817-1887)	(1821-1895)	(1823-1902)

Plate 46 *St Agatha's Church, Portsmouth.*

Plate 47 *Seecham Farm, now called Seecham Manor, the Alvechurch home to at least three generations of the Holbeche family.*

Chapter Six

The Holbeche Family of Sutton Coldfield

ONE OF the last members of the Holbeche family to live in Fillongley was Thomas Holbeche (1772-1848). He was the brother of Aemillian Holbeche of Slowley Hill near Fillongley. Thomas Holbeche was articled to a solicitor in Coleshill but at the age of twenty two he moved to Sutton Coldfield. He rented rooms at the Old School House, Church Yard at the top of Trinity Hill. In the following year he completed his education and was appointed as a solicitor in the High Court of Chancery. He then joined a Mr Croxall in his thriving legal business. At the age of twenty six he joined Sutton Coldfield Corporation and in 1802 he married Sarah Gamble. By this time he was a Warden of Sutton Coldfield and established his own legal practice which grew to be Holbeche, Son & Willoughby. At the time of his marriage he moved to Ivy House in the High Street. His first child Sarah was born there, this was the first of the couple's fifteen children. At this time the population of Sutton Coldfield was about 3,000 souls. Sutton Coldfield was soon to grow into a large town and the Holbeche family were to play an important part in this development as they oversaw this growth as officers of the council.

The growing number of children in the family saw Thomas and Sarah Holbeche soon looking for a larger home. They were offered by the Rev. John Riland, Rector of Holy Trinity Church, the Old Rectory for £1,700. This they accepted. The Old Rectory was also known as 1-3 Coleshill Street and along with it came a pew in the church. Thomas Holbeche retired from business in 1841 but in the same year he became Chairman to the Aston Board of Guardians. His place in the family firm was taken by his son Vincent (1806-1867). In 1845 he married Emma, the daughter of Edward Addenbrooke of The Lea, Herefordshire and of Kingswinford House, Staffs. Vincent Holbeche also served the town of Sutton Coldfield as Deputy Steward to the Warden & Society and when it was incorporated he became the first town clerk of Sutton Coldfield. The Holbeche interest in family and general history continued with this branch of the family. Some of Vincent's unmarried sisters recorded in detail their life at Sutton Coldfield. In particular Helen Holbeche (1821-1895) and Sarah Holbeche (1803-1882) who with other unmarried sisters made their home in Warwick during their later life. In 1885 Helen Holbeche recorded her thoughts on the servants that the family had employed.

> Servants three score years ago were a race worth remembering, they were Sallys and Bettys and Mollys then. We had a number of Sally cooks who married off to be succeeded by other Sallys. But we had but one Nanny, who became a member of the household on the appearance of the first baby – nursed all fifteen – and some of the second generation and died in our midst, leaving all her savings amounting to a few hundred pounds amongst her children whom she nursed.

Vincent's son, Richard also recorded his thoughts concerning his early life in Sutton Coldfield. Richard Holbeche (1850-1914) when young was considered to be no scholar. He was educated at Sandhurst and became a major in the Royal Munster Fusiliers. He saw active service and recorded his experiences in his, *Personal Recollections of the Upper Burma Campaign 1886-7*. He rose to the rank of Lieutenant Colonel. When he retired he worked for the St John's Ambulance Brigade and became involved in sending parcels to the soldiers fighting in the Boer War. He was later appointed librarian of the Order and joined with W.K. Riland Bedford in writing several works on the history of the Knights of St John. W.K. Riland Bedford had been at one time the Rector of Holy Trinity Church in

Sutton Coldfield. Richard Holbeche was honoured shortly before his death in 1914 by being made a knight of the order.[i]

Richard's brother, Edward Addenbrooke Holbeche left home in 1861 at the age of fourteen. He seems to have had a lust for travelling for he later emigrated to New Zealand and became a captain for the New Zealand Shipping Company. He died in 1887 in a fire on board his ship. His son, Vincent Aemillian Holbeche was born in 1886 and returned to Europe as part of New Zealand's army sent to fight in France during the First World War. He was a farmer and enlisted in the Auckland Infantry Regiment on 26th June 1916. He rose to the rank of sergeant but sadly was killed in action on the 18th October 1917.

Another of Richard's brothers was Arthur Oliver Holbeche (1855-1931) who had a distinguished career in medicine. He was a Surgeon-Captain to the Queen's Own Worcestershire Hussars before becoming a senior surgeon to Birmingham General Hospital. He later moved to Malvern and was the Hon. Consulting Surgeon of Malvern Hospital. He, like his brother Richard, became interested in the work of the St John's Ambulance Brigade and became a lecture and examiner for the organisation. Arthur Holbeche was also a Warden of Malvern Priory Church.[ii]

---

[i]   This branch of the family left copious records of their lives at Sutton Coldfield. Through the diligence and hard work of Janet Jordan many of these accounts were photocopied and can be viewed at Sutton Coldfield Library. They include Sarah Holbeche's Diary, *Three Score Years Ago* by Helen Holbeche (1885) and Richard Holbeche, *Personal Recollections of the Upper Burma Campaign, 1886-87* Also see, Janet Jordan, Discovering Holbeche, *Proceedings of the Sutton Coldfield Local History Research Group*, Volume 4: Spring 1997 pp. 15-18.

[ii] *Burke's Landed Gentry*, 1952, Entry for Holbeche of Hillybroom, pp. 1255-1259.

Plate 48 The Old Rectory, Coleshill Street, Sutton Coldfield.
This was the home of the Holbeche family after their move from Fillongley.

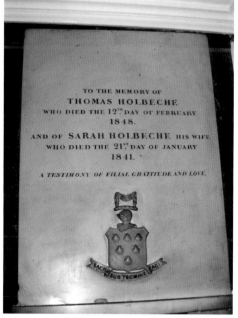

Plate 49 Holy Trinity Church,
Sutton Coldfield.

Plate 50 The monument to Thomas and Sarah
Holbeche, Holy Trinity Church, Sutton Coldfield.

Plate 51 The tiled memorial to Vincent, Emma and Edward Addenbrooke Holbeche, Holy Trinity Church, Sutton Coldfield.

Plate 52 The memorial to Thomas Vincent Holbeche, Holy Trinity Church, Sutton Coldfield.

Plate 53 The memorial in arts and crafts brass to Lt Col Richard Holbeche, Holy Trinity Church, Sutton Coldfield.

Chapter Seven

Matthew Holbeche Bloxam and his Family

ONE GROUP of descendants of the Holbeche family clearly shows the family's deep interest in history, antiquarian matters and religion. These are members of the Bloxam family. Matthew Holbeche Bloxam was born in Rugby on the 12th May 1805. His father was the Rev. Richard Rouse Bloxam, D.D. who was rector of Brinklow, vicar of Bulkington and a master at Rugby School. His mother Anne was the sister of the painter Sir Thomas Lawrence. Richard Rouse Bloxam was the great grandson of Anthony Bloxam (b.1684-1752) of Aston-Subedge who had married Sarah Holbeche the daughter of Matthew Holbeche of Meriden Hall. Richard and Elizabeth Bloxam had six sons and all attended Rugby School.

Matthew Holbeche Bloxam is reported to have been a dull, plodding pupil. However, by the time he left Rugby he had developed a deep interest in history and a great love for his old school. When he was seventeen Bloxam went to work in a solicitor's office in Rugby. The solicitor was George Harris who had an interest in history and probably encouraged his pupil in his antiquarian researches. Bloxam soon developed interests in architectural history, archaeology and the natural sciences including astronomy. Matthew Holbeche Bloxam qualified as a solicitor and appears to have been a success in his profession and still found time for his antiquarian pursuits. As a solicitor's clerk he had to visit countless churches in the county of Warwickshire.

Bloxam held several local Rugby offices. He was clerk of the Rugby petty sessions from 1831 until 1871, he officiated sometimes as deputy registrar of the county court, was a member of the local board from 1855 to 1863 and audited the Rugby Union accounts from 1836 until the appointment of district auditors. He never married and this, perhaps, allowed him that extra time for his huge range of antiquarian studies and writings. His first book was *The Principles of Gothic Architecture* which was published in 1829. It was a short volume of seventy-nine pages written in a question and answer form. Under the later title *of The Principles of Gothic Ecclesiastical Architecture* the book was added to and improved through several editions. The earlier format was replaced by a narrative style. The eleventh and final edition was issued in 1882 and it had grown to three volumes. Before 1882 no less than 17,000 copies of this volume had been sold. This being due to its pocket size, cheapness and clear text. The book was also well illustrated by good woodcut illustrations, the work of Thomas Orlando Sheldon Jewitt (1799-1869), based on his own and Bloxam's drawings. Bloxam also wrote about 200 papers based on his knowledge of over 10,000 churches. He was a member of the Oxford Architectural Society, an honorary member of the Ecclesiological Society and was elected fellow of the Society of Antiquaries in 1863. His advice on historical and ecclesiastical matters was frequently sought and Bloxam was happy to share his knowledge with fellow scholars.

As well as architecture Matthew Holbeche Bloxam was interested in the monuments and effigies to be found in churches. He was very interested in the costume and armour depicted as well as the history of the people commemorated in stone and alabaster. This prompted him to write *A Glimpse of the Monumental Architecture and Sculpture of Great Britain* which was printed by his friend Thomas Combe of Leicester. In 1841 he began work on a second edition of this volume. Thomas Combe, now at the Oxford University Press had 176 pages set in type and these pages were printed. By this time books had been published which superseded his original work and Bloxam realised that the volume required considerable correction. He therefore relinquished all ideas of proceeding with this book and distributed the completed pages to his friends. This uncompleted work he named, *Fragmenta Sepulchralia* and it has some importance for in its pages are recorded Bloxam's own discoveries in the Midlands.

In 1844 one of Bloxam's most important works began to appear. This is generally known as *The Churches of Warwickshire*. The historical side of this publication was written by the Rev. William Staunton, the famous Birmingham historian. It was issued in parts, the 12th appearing in 1857. This was the last owing to the death of Staunton. As well as his antiquarian works Matthew Holbeche Bloxam was passionately interested in the history of Rugby, both town and school. He loved the school that he attended and regularly attended the Sunday afternoon school chapel services. He gave athletic prizes for the younger boys, presented gifts annually on the occasion of his birthday, read papers to the Natural History Society, contributed articles to the school magazines *Meteor* and *Leaflet* and encouraged any boy who showed an interest in archaeology. His writings on the town and school were collated by W.H. Payne Smith and published posthumously as *Rugby: the School and Neighbourhood* (1889). Matthew Holbeche Bloxam was the only source concerning the origins of Rugby Football at the school. He recorded the fact that William Webb Ellis handled the ball during a Rugby School match in 1823 and this form of the game was completely different from football when he left the school in 1821. Writers have claimed that Bloxam perpetuated a myth but the story has stuck and now every four years the rugby playing nations compete in the World Cup with the winners receiving the William Webb Ellis Trophy.

Matthew Holbeche Bloxam enjoyed a healthy constitution until weakened by bronchitis late in 1887. After paralytic seizures he died at Rugby on 24 April 1888. He was described in his obituary as 'the most amiable and, at the same time, the most modest of men'. On the 27 April Bloxam was buried, Rugby School and the parish church lowered their flags to half-mast, blinds were drawn in most homes and the tradesmen closed their shops. At his own request he was buried near a yew tree in the churchyard of St Michael and All Angels, Brownsover, near Rugby. He left Rugby School the choice of his extensive library and his personal papers. He also gave the school his collection of antiquities made up of ancient armour, swords and Greek helmets. Rugby School also received several paintings from his collection.[i]

M.H. Bloxam's brother, John Rouse Bloxam (1807-1891) possessed similar interests in religion and antiquarian matters. After attending Rugby school he proceeded to Worcester College, Oxford where he held a bible clerkship. From

1830 to 1835 he held a demyship at Magdalen College, Oxford, obtaining an honorary fourth class in classics in 1831 and graduating BA in 1832. He was ordained deacon by the Bishop of Oxford in 1832 and priest in 1833 and took further degrees of MA in 1835, BD in 1843 and DD in 1847.

In July 1832 J.R. Bloxam was a chaplain and classical master in the private school at Wyke House, near Brentford and from 1833 to 1836 he was second master at Bromsgrove School. In 1836 he returned to Magdalen College having been elected a probationer fellow. He continued at Magdalen until 1862 and among the college offices he held were bursar, vice-president, and librarian (1851-1862), though he never was a tutor. In 1837 he was appointed a curate to J.H. Newman at Littlemore, Oxfordshire. This gave him the opportunity to promote his ideas on the revival of ceremonial in the Church of England. J.R. Bloxam caused a scandal in 1839 when it was reported that he had bowed to the host during the celebration of mass during a visit to Alton Towers, the seat of the Roman Catholic Earl of Shrewsbury. This forced him to resign his curacy at Littlemore. He corresponded with others of a like mind on the possibility of a reunion of the Anglican and Roman Churches. Bloxam was an early member of the Oxford Society for Promoting the Study of Gothic Architecture founded in 1839. Through this he became a friend and patron of A.W. Pugin and obtained for him the commission for a new gateway at Magdalen College. Pugin must have gathered much information regarding gothic architecture from the Bloxam brothers. In 1845 Newman tried to persuade J.R. Bloxam to become a Roman Catholic but this he resisted although the two men were close friends right up to the death of Newman.

He published several papers on the history of the college. Bloxam was particularly interested in the choral tradition of the college and claimed to have been responsible from 1844 for a more dignified celebration of the May Day custom of singing a hymn on the tower of Magdalen College. In fact he is a prominent figure in Holman Hunt's painting of the ceremony first exhibited in 1891. While at Magdalen he compiled a biographical register of members of the college. Seven volumes of this series were published between 1853 and 1881. J.R. Bloxam also compiled a bibliography of the works published by members of the college. It was said that he carried out this task to refute Edward Gibbon's remarks about the idleness of the Magdalen fellows.

In February 1862 Bloxam was appointed by his college to the vicarage of Upper Beeding, near Steyning in Sussex and in the following year resigned his fellowship. He was acknowledged in later life as, 'the grandfather of all Ritualists'. By the 1880s many of the revivals pioneered by Bloxam had become widely accepted within the Church of England. Bloxam, who never married, died at The Priory, Upper Beeding on 21 January 1891 and was buried in Beeding churchyard.[ii]

Another brother to show a deep interest in religion was Andrew Bloxam (1801-1878). After his education at Rugby School he went to St John's College, Cambridge. In 1820 he moved to Worcester College, Oxford where he later became a Fellow. After graduating in 1824 Bloxam became the naturalist on board HMS Blonde where his brother was the chaplain. The ship transported the bodies of the King and Queen of the Hawaiian Islands back to their homeland. The royal family had made a visit to Britain but had contracted a disease that killed them both. The voyage lasted eighteen months and during the ship's journey a large number of specimens were collected which were later deposited in the British Museum. Andrew Bloxam, while in the Hawaiian Islands, must also have collected some stone artefacts for in the long list of Mathew Holbeche Bloxam's published papers on local history is one exotic example on stone tools of the Pacific Islands.

When Andrew Bloxam returned from the voyage he took holy orders. From 1839 to 1871 he served as priest in charge of Twycross, Leicestershire and from 1871 to 1878 was rector of Harborough Magna, Warwickshire. Bloxam continued his interest in natural history. He has been described as an all-round naturalist although he himself claimed to be no more than a 'holiday botanist'. He contributed to several regional natural histories of the Midlands and he was a corresponding member of the Birmingham Natural History and Microscopical Society. He died at Harborough Magna in February 1878 at the age of seventy-six.[iii]

---

[i] For accounts of his life see, Phillip B. Chatwin, Incidents in the Life of Matthew Holbeche Bloxam, *Dugdale Society Occasional Papers*, No 13, 1959. Rev. W.H. Payne Smith, *Rugby, The School and Neighbourhood*, Collected and Arranged from the Writings of the Late Matthew Holbeche Bloxam O.R., F.S.A. (1889), pp. xvii-xxxiii. *NDNB* (2004-2005), Libby Horner, Entry for Mathew Holbeche Bloxam.

[ii] *NDNB* (2004-2005), M.C. Curthoys, Entry for John Rouse Bloxam.

[iii] *NDNB* (2004-2005), B.D. Jackson & Rev. Giles Hudson, Entry for Andrew Bloxam.

Matthew Holbeche Bloxam

At. 75. May 12 – 1880.

Engraved by W. Ridgway from a Photograph by C... Vaught...

Plate 54 *Matthew Holbeche Bloxam (1805-1888).*

Chapter Eight

The Holbech Family of Mollington and Farnborough

ONE IMPORTANT branch of the Holbech family moved to the border of Warwickshire and Oxfordshire during the seventeenth century. This branch was founded by Ambrose Holbech who was the great grandson of William Holbech of the White House, Fillongley. He was baptised at Fillongley in 1596. He rose to become a well known lawyer and by 1629 had settled in the village of Mollington. In 1662 Anthony Woodhull the elder and his son Anthony conveyed the manor and the main estate in Mollington to Ambrose and his son of the same name. At this time part of the estate lay in Warwickshire and part in Oxfordshire. In 1895 the county boundary was changed to bring the whole of Mollington into Oxfordshire.

Ambrose Holbech married Joan, daughter of Thomas Holloway of Copredy and had seven children. His son, Ambrose was also a notable lawyer and according to his monument in Mollington Church was 'very eminent in ye Law particularly in ye art of conveyancing which he practiced with great integrity'. Ambrose Holbech the younger died in 1700 aged sixty-nine. It must have been a lucrative profession for Ambrose Holbech had procured further estates at Radstone, Northamptonshire and nearby Farnborough by the time of his death. He must have been a well known and important member of the legal profession for his daughter Sarah married Sir Thomas Powys of Lilford Hall, Northamptonshire. Powys was appointed solicitor-general in 1686 and received a knighthood, in the next year he was appointed attorney-general. In 1711 he purchased Lilford Hall. He died in 1719 aged seventy. His life and marriage to Sarah Holbech are recorded on a very large monument which was at one time in Lilford Church. This church was demolished in the eighteenth century and the tomb and monument moved to nearby Achurch. Sir Thomas Powys and Sarah had six children, namely Thomas, Edward, Ambrose, Sarah, Anne and Jane. The monument in the floor of the church at Achurch to Thomas Powys includes the Holbech coat of arms with the shells. This monument seems to have been produced by the same mason who completed the Holbech monumental slabs in the church at Mollington. Many of the monuments at Mollington were commissioned by Finetta Holbech who died in 1758 and was the youngest daughter of Ambrose Holbech the younger. The Lilford family still own and occupy Lilford Hall and one group of descendants includes the writers John Cowper Powys and Llewellyn Powys.

The Mollington estates tended to be the seats of the junior members of the family as the Farnborough estate was developed and grew in importance. Ambrose Holbech's eldest son, William married Elizabeth, the daughter and co-heiress of William Alington of London. William Holbech eventually succeeded to the three properties in 1701 and died in 1717.

Ambrose Holbech of Mollington had bought Farnborough in 1684 from the Raleigh family. It was his son, William who probably began to improve the house after his marriage in 1692. His arms and initials and that of his wife, Elizabeth Alington appear on the richly worked ceiling of the staircase. It is probable that they also rebuilt the west side of the house. Their son, William, succeeded his father in 1717 and until his death had much time to adapt the rest of the house and to landscape the grounds. He rebuilt Farnborough Hall and landscaped the grounds in the period around 1740. William was known as a connoisseur and was much influenced by a long trip he made to Italy. Family tradition has it that after being disappointed in love he travelled to Italy and lived there for over ten years. He returned to England in about 1734 much influenced by his time in Italy. He brought from Europe three Panini paintings and two of the Canalettos that hung at one time in the dining room. The sculptured busts that are now in the hall and staircase were bought during his time in Italy. William Holbech wanted Farnborough Hall to resemble the houses he had visited and admired in Italy. His main building work was carried out in the 1740s. The rich, almost, Italian exterior was achieved by the use of the local ochre coloured Hornton stone. During this time the stucco decoration in the hall, staircase and dining room was completed. William Holbech also spent much time, energy and money on the landscaping at Farnborough. Its chief feature was a raised terrace rising in an arc from the house and running for three-quarters of a mile. Incorporated on this terrace are an oval pavilion, an Ionic temple and an obelisk. Another temple had vanished by the end of the eighteenth century.

William Holbech did not marry and when he died in 1771 he was succeeded by his nephew, also named William. He was the son of Hugh Holbech who had accompanied William Holbech on his trip to Italy. Hugh Holbech lived at Mollington and had married Catherine, daughter of Col Robert Cornewall. William Holbech became MP for Banbury in 1792 and Deputy Lieutenant of the county in 1796. He married Anne, the daughter of William Woodhouse of Lichfield. Their son was another William who married Lucy the daughter of Oldfield Bowles of North Aston. They had ten children but it was their third son Charles who succeeded to the estates in 1856. He married Laura Harriette, sister of Sir George Armytage of Kirklees Park in Yorkshire. Charles became a priest and held the living at Farnborough, later becoming Archdeacon of Coventry. He sold the Radstone estate and spent a great deal of money restoring St Botolph's church at Farnborough. This included building a new aisle and spire to the designs of Gilbert Scott. Another one of his projects was to build a new road to the village of Avon Dassett.

Archdeacon Holbech had five sons and four daughters. The eldest son, Walter became a colonel in the King's Royal Rifles and later one of HM Royal Bodyguards. Another son, William Arthur Holbech became Bishop of St Helena and Tristan Da Cunha in the South Atlantic. The youngest son, Hugh, took Holy Orders and later became a canon in the diocese of Coventry. Walter Holbech died before his father. Farnborough therefore was inherited by his eldest son William.[i] During his minority the estate was managed by Canon Hugh Holbech who took a great interest in his family's history and often corresponded with Gerald

Holbeche who in the 1940s was trying to unravel the history of all the branches of the family.

William Holbech died in October 1914. He was killed in the First World War serving with the Scots Guards. His brother, Ronald inherited the property and he married in 1915. His wife was Catherine, the youngest daughter of Sir Leigh Hoskyns. Ronald Holbech's eldest son was Edward Ambrose Holbech and he served with distinction with the RAF during the Second World War during which time he was awarded the DFC. Sadly he was killed in an accident on VJ Day 1945. He had by this time made a settlement on his only child Anne and his brother Geoffrey.

Farnborough Hall continues to be occupied by members of the Holbech family. Most of the estate was sold in 1948 following extensive damage in the gales of 1947 The house with 344 acres passed to the National Trust in 1960.[ii] The Holbech family continue to hold this famous house on a lease and Farnborough Hall is open to the public on a regular basis. The honey coloured walls of this attractive house continues to hold over 300 years of Holbech family history.

---

[i] *Burke's Landed Gentry* (1952), Entry for Holbech of Farnborough, pp. 1254-1255.
[ii] *Farnborough Hall*, National Trust Guide (1999), pp. 1-30.

Plate 55 *All Saints Church, Mollington.*

Plate 56 *The monument to Ambrose and Sarah Holbech, All Saints Church, Mollington.*

Plate 57 *The monument to Ambrose Holbech who died in 1739, All Saints Church, Mollington.*

Plate 58 A tablet erected to the memory of Elizabeth Holbech, All Saints Church, Mollington.

Plate 59 The floor monument to Finetta Holbech, All Saints Church, Mollington.

Plate 60 Farnborough Hall, Warwickshire, home to the Holbech family.

Plate 61 St Botolph's Church, Farnborough.

Plate 62 *Monuments to military members of the Holbech family in the graveyard, St Botolph's Church, Farnborough.*

Plate 63 *Monuments to members of the Holbech family, St Botolph's Church, Farnborough.*

Plate 64 *The monument to William Holbech and Elizabeth Holbech (Alington), St Botolph's Church, Farnborough.*

Plate 65 *Tablet memorials to Charles W Holbech and William A Holbech, priests and bishops in the Church of England, St Botolph's Church, Farnborough.*

Plate 66 *A tablet memorial to Hugh Holbech, St Botolph's Church, Farnborough.*

Plate 67 *The parish church at Achurch, Northamptonshire.*

Plate 68 The magnificent monument to members of the Powys family of Lilford Park at Achurch.

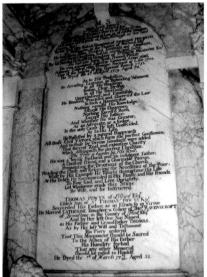

Plate 69 The text of the Powys monument which records the marriage of Sir Thomas Powys and Sarah Holbech.

Plate 70 The floor monument to Sir Thomas Powys at Achurch. He was the son of Sarah Holbech and his coat of arms include the Holbech shells.

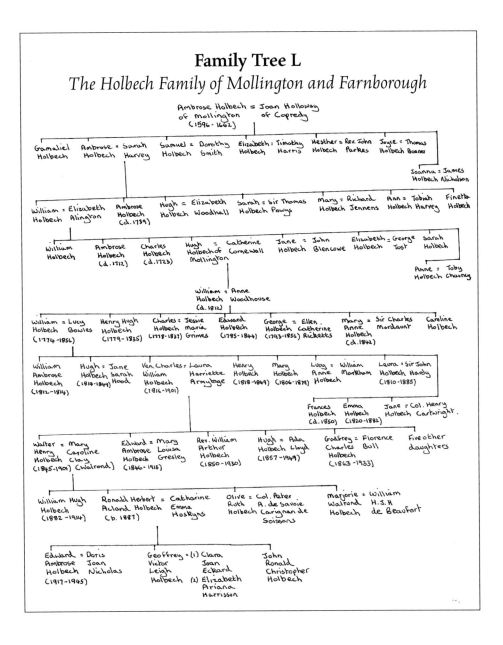

Family Tree L

The Holbech Family of Mollington and Farnborough

Appendix One

Holbeche Monumental Inscriptions at St Mary & All Saints Church, Fillongley

One

This monument was erected by the direction of Mrs Mary Holbeche, Relict of Aemillian Holbeche, sometime of Maxstoke Priory, Gent, in memory of Thomas the son of Martin Holbeche of Fillongley Gent who died on the 29th day of Dec 1744 aged 70 years.

Also of Mary wife of the said Thomas Holbeche who died 26th day of April 1700 aged 25 years. The said Aemillian Holbeche son of the said Thomas and Mary Holbeche who died the 21st day of January 1760 aged 60 years which Mary wife of the said Aemillian Holbeche died the 11th January 1772 aged 74 years. Aemillian and Mary Holbeche had issue six children:

Mary died 22nd September 1728 aged 13 weeks
Elizabeth wife of Revd John Blyth, Rector of Bagington
Ann died 8th October 1731 aged 26 weeks
Thomas died 8th October 1735 aged 37 weeks 3 days
Aemillian and Thomas

Two

Near this place was interred Anne Daniel widow and Elizabeth her only surviving daughter who was marryed to Thomas Holbeche of this parish, gent and were both buryed here. They had three sons Pawlett, Thomas and William who all dyed unmarryed and were all buryed underneath: and one daughter Mary who marryed to ye Right Hon Edward, Lord Leigh, Baron of Stoneleigh by whom this monument was erected in a pious regard to the memory of her said Grandmother, Mother, Father and three brothers.

A.D. 1725

Three

It was recorded in the eighteenth century that there were Holbeche monumental inscriptions on flat stones in the chancel of Fillongley church. They were recorded as,

HERE LYETH THE BODY OF THOMAS HOLBECHE
OF THE PARISH GENT. WHO DEPARTED
THIS LIFE THE 10th Day OF AUGUST 1705.
Aged 66.

Here lyeth the body of Elizabeth Holbeche, wife of Thomas Holbeche Gent. who departed this life June the 30. 1718. Aged 66. She gave a very rich pulpit cloth and Cushion of Crimson velvet, with her arms curiously embroider'd thereon, with the two first letters of her Name, and the day of her burial.

Here lyeth the body of Paulet Holbeche his eldest son, who departed this life 24. March 1702. Aetatis fuae 25.

... Thomas Holbeche 2d. son, who departed this life 28. June 1699.

William Holbeche youngest son, 18. May 1703. Aetat fuae 20.

MARY WIFE OF THOMAS HOLBECH
OF FILLONGLEY HALL, WHO DEPARTED
THIS LIFE 26 APRILL 1700.
AETATIS SUAE 25.

Several of the Holbeches of the White House lie also buried in the same aisle.

Appendix Two

Holbech Monumental Inscriptions in the Church of St Alphege, Solihull

One (Translated from the Latin)
In this chapel of S. Catherine, the ancient vault of the Holbeches of Bentley and Solihull, William Holbech, of Bentley Heath, gent, a man of great kindliness and industry, who died in the year of our salvation, 1712, in the 76th year of his age, and by his last testament willed, in the first place, that this Tablet (beneath which he himself lies, together with his wife, Maria Davis) be dedicated to the honour of his Father's sister, Elizabeth, (widow of William, daughter of Thomas, and sister of Barnabas, all Holbeches of Bentley Heath,) by whom he had been brought up and who is buried here. The Testator also willed that he himself should be represented by one of the figures placed on the cornice above, and his aunt by the other, and that she should be commemorated after this manner:

'Here lyeth one, a pattern true, in life of kindly heart,
A type of Christian piety, Elizabeth the wise;
The doleful urn now holds the ashes of her mortal part:
The happy soul, releas'd, has flown to realms beyond the skies.'

"Memorable is the family of the Bentley Holbeches, which rests in this vault, originating, as I find, at Whitehouse, Fillongley, about the year 1500, and continuing in the direct line unto the sixth generation, a very rare occurrence:

Great-great-great-Grandfather – Richard, (son of Thomas Holbech, of Whitehouse, Fillongley, Esquire) – 1551
Great-great-Grandfather – Barnabas – 1569 (1586)
Great-grandfather – Thomas (his daughter is the above mentioned Elizabeth) – 1634
Grandfather – Barnabas (his son is the above mentioned William, the Testator) – 1645

Father – Thomas (Father of John, the Executor of William's will) –
1712, aged 50
Son – Thomas (BA, unmarried) – 1692

"But far more distinguished is the very ancient family itself, which probably derived its name from Holbech (Holbeck) a town in Zealand, which lies across the sea opposite the County of Lincoln, for it is stated that it came over here with Canute, King of the Danes; though some people are inclined to think it is of Saxon origin. It then divided into various branches, of which some have become extinct, but others are still flourishing, and of these the Solihull-Bentley branch, here in Warwickshire, is not the least important. Yet all claim as their earliest ancestor and founder (until an earlier come to light) Oliver Holbech, of Holbech, who lived more than 460 years ago, (for he was the contemporary of Henry III, who reigned in the thirteenth century), and fixed the seat of his fortunes on the estuary of Holland, a district of Lincolnshire, called by Ptolemy, 'Metaris aestuarium,' [i.e The Wash,] and married a lady of noble birth as the family arms here represented, impaled with those of her husband, indicate. [The arms are engraved here viz.: Dexter, Vert, 5 escalops Argent; Sinister, Sable, a pile, Or.] This family produced men famous in the arts of peace and war. Laurence Holbech shone out in the fourteenth century as the wonder of the rude times in which he lived, and died about the tenth year of the following century; he was trained at the Monastery of Ramsey, in Huntingdonshire, and was the first Englishman to compile a Hebrew lexicon; he was, moreover, a consummate master of other languages and learned arts, and his native town Holbech in Lincolnshire, is as proud of him as Rotterdam is of its Erasmus.

"Contemporary with Laurence was David Holbech, Esquire. It was to his intercession alone that Owen Glendower owed his life and safety when he was defeated and taken prisoner by King Henry IV after five years' desperate rebellion. This Owen had such confidence in his own strength that, (although he was worsted), he dared to challenge to single combat that consummate fighter and brilliant general, Richard Beauchamp, Earl of Warwick during whose life-time the cause of England flourished in France, but on whose death it began to decline.

"At the siege of the French cities, Montreuil and Boulogne, in 1544, Thomas Holbech, a very brave man, carried off the prize from his comrades, for King Henry VIII added to his family arms, which consisted of five shells, three golden lions' heads to be borne on an Azure Ground, as a special reward for the valour he displayed.

"In 1547, after King Edward VI had been crowned, Henry Holbech, one of the compilers of the solemn prayers still in use in the Church of England, [viz.; The First Prayer Book of Edward VI] was consecrated Bishop of Lincoln; a man of great reputation but varied fortune, he was made a Doctor of Divinity at Cambridge.

"In the same place there flourished, lately, in the reign of William III, Thomas Holbech, Vice-Chancellor of the University and Doctor in Divinity. The last of the band is Thomas Holbech, the Bachelor of Arts mentioned above, compiler of the genealogical tree of the Holbeches of the Meriden branch, and author of a Handbook on Heraldry, chiefly with reference to his own line, by which small works he has earned for himself the light and immorality which he bestowed upon his family.

"Concerning John Holbech, brother of Thomas, as yet surviving, the stone below will speak, and the accompanying epitaph, to be erected if the fates permit.

[*On stone below*]: "John Holbech, Esquire, son of Thomas, brother of Thomas, the Executor of the Will made by William, his Uncle, caused this Tablet to be made in the year 1726.

'The glory of the Holbech name is now, at last, restor'd;
For evermore shall live the fame of its ancestral lord;
T'is good to seek the well-earned praise of kin and Fatherland!
See, now, how joy lights up the faces of the spirit-band,
John's kindred, when they see the monument which his love gave,
And know that they shall ne'er be cover'd quite by Lethe's wave.'

[*On the parallel panel*]: "Outside the North wall of this Chapel are deposited the remains of John Short, who after many years spent in the practice of medicine and a few in honourable leisure, at length quietly entered into rest, as he had lived, in Christ, on the 2nd day of April, 1831, in his 92nd year of his age. He left to survive him six sons – John, Charles, Edward, Richard, Robert, Thomas; three daughters – Jane, Maria, Elizabeth; and several grand-children.

"In the same grave are laid the remains of Jane Short, for more than sixty-three years a faithful wife and sweet mother, who laid aside mortality in the hope of the Crown of Life on the 15th day of December, 1831, in the 86th year of her age.

Her Father – Richard Mashiter, Clerk 1713 – 1769

Her Brothers – Edward Holbeche Mashiter, 1743 – 1782, Richard Mashiter, 1744 – 1778

Her Mother – Mary, died 1748

Her Grandfather – Anthony Holbech, esquire; (the son of Thomas, the elder, commemorated on the next slab) 1662 – 1738

Her Grandmother – Jane (daughter of John Parsons, Knight), died 1753

"The bodies of these are buried in the Chapel.

"Near his parents rests the above mentioned Richard Short who, after being long afflicted with a very severe illness, died, more seasonably to himself than his friends, on the 2nd day of February, 1837, in the 60th year of his age. Their sorrowing relations have caused this monument to be erected to the best of Parents and a deeply lamented Brother."

Two

"For that divers of his Ancestors since 1514 and that many of his near'st relations, lie here interr'd; to protect henceforth ye quiet of ye bones, they having long unguarded lain, freely beneath in trust are plac'd six guardian figured stones thro' debt of honour duly laid by J. Holbech of Whitehal, Esq, 1745."

Three

"In 1640 Edward Holbech gave to 4 Trustees, their heirs and assigns £3 a year out of his 'Good Hart' land by them to be disbursed on Christmas and Midsummer Eve yearly, to ye poor and needy people of ye Parish, for ever. See copy in ye Chest. Set up by J. Holbech of Whitehal, Esq., 1745."

Source, Robert Pemberton, *Solihull and its Church* (Exeter,1905), pp. 177-185.

Appendix Three

Abstract of the Will of Leonard Holbeche of Fillongley, 13th August 1546, Proved 30th April 1547

To be buried in the Church of Fillongley

To the High Altar, 8d

To the reparation and maintenance of the church goods, a tablecloth of flax

I give 5s to be spent in wax at my burial

I give 11s to be spent in meat and drink upon my neighbours and poor people on the day of my burial

To the poor people of Arley, Astley and Corley, 5s

To Elizabeth Wood, William Holbeche son of Barnaby, John Brearley son of Elizabeth Brearley and to Leonard Osmond son of Richard Osmond and to William Holbeche son of John Holbeche Junior, to every of them a lamb of this year and to all other godchildren 4d a piece

To the reparation of the highway, there is a most need, 6s 8d

To Thomas Eddes, a jacket

I will that Agnes my wife shall have 8 kine, a bull and a mare

I will that Margaret Perkins be paid her part of her legacy of her father's gift out of my whole goods

Residue to Agnes my wife and to John Holbeche, my son equally between them whom I make my Executors.

Witnesses, William Holbeche, Gent, Sir John Nycolson and Sir Robert Wheatley, priests with others.

Source, Warwickshire Record Office, Holbeche Family Papers, 1680/632

Bibliography

Manuscript Sources
Birmingham Reference Library
Crowder & Smallwood Collection
Bodleian Library, Oxford
Tanner Collection
Centre For Kentish Studies, Maidstone
Sackville Collection
Guildhall Library, London
Minutes of the Worshipful Company of Distillers
Shakespeare Birthplace Trust Records Office
Leigh of Stoneleigh Collection
Sutton Coldfield Library
Photocopies of Holbeche Diaries etc.
Warwickshire Record Office, Warwick
Bree of Allesley and Beausale Estate Papers
Fetherston-Dilke of Maxstoke Collection
Holbeche Family Papers

Printed Sources
Alcock, N.W., *People at Home, Living in a Warwickshire Village, 1500-1800* (Chichester, 1993)
Agutter, Doreen M.K., *Meriden: Its People and Houses* (ND)
Bendall, Sarah, Brooke Christopher & Collinson Patrick, *A History of Emmanuel College, Cambridge* (Woodbridge, 1999)
Berlin, Michael, *The Worshipful Company of Distillers, A Short History* (Chichester, 1996)
Bickley, W.B. (Ed), *The Register of the Guild of Knowle* (Walsall, 1894)
Bradney, Sir Joseph, *A History of Monmouthshire, Vol I, The Hundred of Abergavenny* (1906)
Burke's Landed Gentry (1952)
Calendar of Inquisitions, Edward II
Chatwin, Philip, Incidents in the Life of Matthew Holbeche Bloxam, *Dugdale Society Occasional Papers No 13* (1959)
Craze, Michael, *A History of Felsted School 1564-1947* (Ipswich, 1955)

Davies, W. Eileen, *Beauchamps* (Studley, 1985)

Denton, Barry, *Only in Heaven, The Life and Campaigns of Sir Arthur Hesilrige, 1601-1661* (Sheffield, 1997)

Dugdale, William, *The Antiquities of Warwickshire* (1656 & 2nd edition, 1730)

Farnborough Hall, National Trust Guide (1999)

Gravett, Christopher, *Towton 1461, England's Bloodiest Battle* (Botley, 2003)

Johnson, H.C. & Williams, N.J. (Eds), *Warwick County Records, Vol IX, Quarter Sessions Records Easter 1690 to Michaelmas 1696* (Warwick, 1964)

Jorden, Janet, Discovering Holbeche, *Proceedings of the Sutton Coldfield Local History Research Group*, Vol 4 (1997)

Lander, J.R., *Crown and Nobility 1450-1509* (1976)

New Dictionary of National Biography (Oxford 2004-5), Curthoys, M.C., Entry for John Rouse Bloxam, Horner, Libby, Entry for Matthew Holbeche Bloxam, Hudson, Giles & Jackson, B.D., Entry for Andrew Bloxam & Larminie, Vivienne, Entry for Martin Holbeche

Parliamentary Papers, An Act for appointing Commissioners to continue the Inquiries concerning Charities in England and Wales for Two Years and from then to the end of the next session of Parliament (1835)

Pemberton, Robert, *Solihull and its Church* (Exeter, 1905)

Platt, Graham, *History of Lincolnshire, Vol IV, Land and People in Medieval Lincolnshire* (Lincoln, 1985)

Ratcliffe, S.C. & Johnson, H.C. *Warwick County Records, Vol II, Quarter Sessions Book, Michelmas 1637 to Epiphany 1650* (Warwick, 1936)

Ratcliffe, S.C. & Johnson, H.C., *Warwick County Records, Vol III, Quarter Sessions Order Book, Easter 1650 to Epiphany 1657* (Warwick, 1938)

Ratcliffe, S.C. & Johnson, H.C., *Warwick County Records, Vol VI, Quarter Sessions, Indictment Book, Easter 1631 to Epiphany 1674* (Warwick, 1941)

Smith, Rev W.H. Payne, *Rugby, the School and its Neighbourhood* (1889)

Ward, Audrey, *Discovering Reigate Priory* (Reigate, 1998)

Warner, Jessica, *Craze, Gin and Debauchery in an Age of Reason* (2003)

Warwickshire Antiquarian Magazine (1859-77)

Webb, Cliff, *London Apprentices, Vol III, Distillers' Company 1659-1811* (1997)

Woodhead, J.R., *The Rulers of London 1660-1689* (1965)

Venn J. & J.A., *Alumni Cantabrigienses, Vol II* (1922)

List of Illustrations

15. Saint Mary's Church, Stow-in-Lindsey.
16. Part of the stone tablet commemorating the Holbech family in Stow church. The five shells can be plainly seen as can the three lions granted for valour.
17. Saint Augustine's Church, Dodderhill, Droitwich.
18. A memorial tablet to the first wife and children of Thomas Holbeche, St Augustine's, Dodderhill.
19. A charity board at St Augustine's Church, Dodderhill. The board shows a bequest settled on the church through Thomas Holbeche's estate.
20. Mary Holbech (1634-1709) of Birchley Hall. She married Sir William Cayley of Brompton, Yorkshire in 1653.
21. Thomas Holbech (1606-1680) of Birchley Hall, Master of Emmanuel College, Cambridge. (By permission of the Master and Fellows of Emmanuel College, Cambridge)
22. The Church of St John the Baptist, St Lawrence and St Anne, Knowle.
23. The Guild House beside the church at Knowle. It was the attractions of membership of the Guild of Knowle that brought the Holbeche family to the Solihull area.
24. Thomas Holbech (d.1692), one of the seventeenth century historians of the family.
25. Anthony Holbech of Bentley Hall (1662-1738). It was his career as a distiller in London that renewed the fortunes of the family.
26. Jane Holbech, wife of Anthony and daughter of Sir John Parsons.
27. The arms of Anthony Holbech taken from an eighteenth century pedigree roll produced for the family. Oxidation has turned the green background colours to blue.
28. The church of St Nicholas Cole Abbey, London. This was the church in London attended by Anthony Holbech and his family. His children were christened here and the church is famous as being the first church built by Wren in London after the Great Fire.
29. Reigate Priory, the home of the Parsons family in the eighteenth century.
30. A rather fanciful depiction of Oliver Holbech which starts the eighteenth century pedigree roll of the family. The gap in the inscription shows where the name de Randes has later been removed.
31. Thomas Holbech (1632-1712), eldest son of Barnaby Holbech.
32. Elizabeth Holbech, wife of Thomas Holbech, daughter of Luke Clapham of Winnal Hall, near Coventry.
33. John Holbech of Whitehall, London (1670-1753).
34. Elizabeth, wife of John Holbech and daughter of John Day of Somerset.
35. The arms of John Holbech from the eighteenth century pedigree roll.
36. Clapham Holbech (d.1739), son of Anthony Holbech and nicknamed 'The Steeple Flyer'.
37. Mary Mashiter, daughter of Anthony Holbech and wife of Dr Richard Mashiter, the headmaster of Solihull Grammar School.
38. Day Holbech (1710-1764), son of John and Elizabeth Holbech. He is dressed as a page to Queen Anne.

66. A tablet memorial to Hugh Holbech, St Botolph's Church, Farnborough.
67. The parish church at Achurch, Northamptonshire.
68. The magnificent monument to members of the Powys family of Lilford Park at Achurch.
69. The text of the Powys monument which records the marriage of Sir Thomas Powys and Sarah Holbech.
70. The floor monument to Sir Thomas Powys at Achurch. He was the son of Sarah Holbech and his coat of arms include the Holbech shells.

FIGURES
1. The arms of the Holbeche/Holbech family.
2A. The arms of some of the families related to the Holbeche family through marriage (Clapham, Dabridgcourt & Leigh).
2B. The arms of some of the families related to the Holbeche family through marriage (Kittermaster, Cayley & Parkyns).
3. Two Holbech coats of arms discovered at Bentley Hall and Widney, Solihull.
4. The signature of Thomas Holbeche of Fillongley. This has been taken from a deed of entail made 14 December, 1612 by Sir Thomas Dilke, Kt, upon the first marriage of his son with the daughter of Sir Edward Devereux, Kt of Castle Bromwich.

FAMILY TREES
A. The Holbech Family of Stow, Lincolnshire
B. The Holbeches of the White House, Fillongley
C. The Holbeches of Fillongley Hall and Slowley Hill
D. The Holbeches of Fillongley
E. The Holbech Family of Birchley Hall
F. The Holbechs of Corley and Stoneleigh
G. The Holbech Family of Solihull
H. The Hollington Family of Alvechurch
I. The Holbeches of Alvechurch
J. The Dolling and Montgomery Descent from the Holbech Family
K. The Holbeches of Sutton Coldfield
L. The Holbech family of Mollington and Farnborough

ABBREVIATIONS USED
B. born
Bapt. baptised
Bur. buried
D. died

Index